Values Begin at Home

Values Begin at Home

Ted Ward

While this book is designed for the reader's personal enjoyment and profit, it is also intended for group study. A Leader's Guide with Victor Multiuse Transparency Masters is available from your local bookstore or from the publisher.

VICTOR BOOKS a division of SP Publications, Inc.

WHEATON, ILLINOIS 60187

Offices also in
Whitby, Ontario, Canada
Amersham-on-the-Hill, Bucks, England

Fourth printing, 1984

Scripture quotations are taken from the *New American Standard Bible*
(NASB), © 1960, 1962, 1968, 1971, 1972, 1973 by the Lockman Foundation,
La Habra, California. Used by permission.

Recommended Dewey Decimal Classification: 248.4
Suggested subject headings: Christian Ethics; Behavior

Library of Congress Catalog Card Number: 76-68855
ISBN: 0-88207-637-X

VICTOR BOOKS
A division of SP Publications, Inc.
                Wheaton, Illinois 60187

Contents

70222

Foreword

In a time of great family consciousness and opportunity, many churches are devoting increasing energies to family ministries. Churches can teach people skills and concepts for healthy marriage and family relationships with greater depth than any other institution. Churches can also offer assistance and support at times of crisis, and have built-in structures for education, enrichment, and problem-solving.

This book has been carefully planned to capitalize on the unique abilities and opportunities churches have to minister to people's needs. Pastors and other church professionals will find this book invaluable for reference and counseling. Though this book stands alone as a valuable resource, materials are provided so that it may be used for group study.

A leader's guide provides thirteen, one-hour, step-by-step plans for studying this book in a group setting. These guides may be used in adult Sunday School, Sunday evening or midweek study series, small informal study groups, and as seminars and workshops in conferences and retreats. These guides include complete study plans, learning activity instructions, visual aids, and suggestions for further investigation and reading.

This book gives reliable and practical solutions to many difficult problems. May God deeply enrich your life and your family as you study and grow.

Preface

Matters of moral judgment are everyone's concern. Therefore, not all books on the subject should be written for experts. Since only a few technical words have been used in this book, teenagers and adults should be able to read and discuss it together. A few of the essential words are listed and defined in the *Glossary*.

The specialized and technical vocabulary of any field serves an important purpose. Experts sometimes seem to use big words in order to lock out newcomers to the field. But the real purpose of the special words is to allow for greater precision in communicating important details of the subject. No scientist can function without a vocabulary of big words, no matter how much he may want to explain things simply.

As a scientific detail becomes more a matter of public concern, the scientist's words become more widely used. Rarely is the technical word changed or dropped; instead, *people* change. What they formerly overlooked, because it didn't make sense, they now talk about with ease.

For example, consider the word *atomic*. Although a few of us in high school in the early 40s struggled to get this word into our vocabulary, in a matter of three months after the bombs fell on Hiroshima and Nagasaki, the football crowds in our little town were cheering for our smallest, toughest halfback, calling him by his new nickname, "Atomic" Martin.

Why did the scientists expect people to understand the word "atomic"? Wouldn't "little bitty speck of matter" be easier? (Notice how inexact this is, and it used five simple words to replace one technical word.) As for *nuclear*, President Eisenhower couldn't even pronounce it! But today, almost every North American uses the word and feels strongly about it—one way or the other.

We know that we live in the atomic age. But what isn't so clear is that we are living in a great age of moral decision. Perhaps never before in the history of humankind have so many people been involved so vitally in making such difficult moral choices. These moral choices are on small matters and large matters. Since tradition is being shaken apart all over the world, people make all sorts of individual moral decisions that were formerly left to tradition and to nonthinking habits.

Since the world has shrunk, a terrorist or careless industrial laborer could touch off a world-smearing cloud of death. We all share in moral responsibilities for and with each other, far beyond the wildest imagination of John Donne, the 17th-century poet who first made the observation that "No man is an island."

We need to gear up for the moral demands of our time. Not long ago, some Christians had little more to talk about in the moral realm then whether or not going to movies is sinful. May God spare us from stumbling over the little matters while the huge issues of truth sweep us toward the hour of judgment. As Christians, we have to find our voices in time. The world is full of difficult moral issues: the right to life, the persecution of minorities, the torture and killing of political prisoners, the selfish misuse of the earth's dwindling resources, and the mindless dash toward mechanization and materialism. When will we get ourselves together? Not until we learn how to think about and how to talk about moral values.

This book does not tell us what to think about particular moral issues, though I have made no special effort to conceal my own positions. Instead, the book is offered as an encouragement for us all to think more carefully about the moral issues around us and about the value choices we make day by day.

My hope and continuing prayer is that the book will help families talk together more about moral issues; and beyond the talking, find ways to act.

"You are the salt of the earth" (Matt. 5:13). Salt must be really salty if it is to have its intended effect.

"You are the light of the world" (Matt. 5:14). No light is intended to be hidden. Its purpose is to enlighten and to enable people to see.   TED WARD

1

What Kinds of Values Are There?

You are a person. As a person, you are a unique cluster of values. No one else is like you!

What is important to you shapes your life. Everything you do shows your values.

What is happiness? What is success? What do you fear? What do you like? What is good? What is bad? What is right? What is wrong? These are *value* questions.

This book is not about ice cream, but that's where we will start to look at the matter of values. Surprised? Don't be. We'll get into more important things, all in good time.

Tastes
Some people prefer chocolate ice cream; some prefer vanilla. Maybe your favorite is strawberry or butter pecan (that's mine). Whatever you choose as your favorite flavor tells something about you. When you say, "My favorite is such and such," or, "I don't like lemon sherbet," you show something about your values. Your tastes in all sorts of things (music, art, clothes, furniture, pets) are part of what makes you the special person that you are.

Values are concerned with little things as well as big things. Whether you prefer chocolate or vanilla ice cream isn't really important. But how you should treat other people is another matter. Your relationships with other people express more important values than your preferences for ice cream flavors.

Preferences for flavors, colors, flowers, brand names, or styles are matters of taste. Tastes are unimportant values, but they add up to a total. Can you think of a man who usually drives a Ford car, wears blue most of the time, wears a floppy jacket, and always orders iced tea? If you know such a person, notice how easy it is to spot him by mentioning four of his tastes. What three or four of your tastes would your friends think of when describing you?

Taken one by one, your tastes are not very important. But all together they add up to the *you* that others know. Very likely you wouldn't want to be known for such simple and unimportant things (tastes probably don't say much about what kind of person you are, as you see yourself), but they are part of what others see. We hope other people look deeper. But when they do, what do they see?

Investments
When Jesus talked about values, He skipped right over the matter of tastes and put His finger on *investments*. What sorts of things you put your money and time into tell something important about you.

Jesus said, "Where your treasure is, there will your heart be also" (Matt. 6:21).

Most people in North America put a lot of money into the house or apartment where they live. They invest in housing because they value having nice places in which to live. Whether buying or renting, investments in housing take a big bite out of a family's income. Housing is an investment and it shows a value.

We buy other things. Some of these purchases we call *necessities*. Others we call *extras* or, more honestly, *luxuries*. The way we spend money shows the values that are basic in our lives.

Many North Americans are called affluent because they

have enough money to buy things they don't need. How do you decide that you really need something? What some people call a *necessity*, others call a *luxury*. Even how we make the distinction between necessities and luxuries tells something about our values. A luxury that we don't have may become a necessity when we see that our neighbors have bought one. How easily we convince ourselves that we *need* things!

Time is like money. You have only so much time in a day. You make choices about how to spend it. The choices tell much about your values.

Decisions and Habits

When we think about how to use time and money, we see how we set the pattern for our lives through our investments. Some investments are decisions and some are habits. We find out how important our values really are when we face an investment decision head-on and make a logical choice. But when we do things as habits, without thinking, we lose part of our self-control.

Jesus said, "Do not lay up for yourselves treasures upon earth, where moth and rust destroy, and where thieves break in and steal" (Matt. 6:19). These words are a warning that some of our decisions can lead to poor investments.

There's good news and bad news about value decisons. The good news is that we have a built-in desire to make our own decisions. The bad news is that we have a tendency to neglect things—even important things. Neglecting to take the responsibility for good decision-making lets a lot of life fall into patterns of habits. We do things not so much because we choose to but because we take the easy way out. It's easiest to act on habits. It saves so much thinking and effort.

Born That Way

The human infant is almost helpless. Compared with many other creatures, we arrive in this world wholly dependent. We are born needing help. We are born needing love and the warmth of affection. Because we are so helpless, we start right out as social creatures, needing to relate to other human beings.

We are born with only a few instincts—to cry out, to breathe, to turn toward warmth, to suck, to swallow. Not a very flattering bag of tricks, but it gets us through the first few months. Then, something else takes over: not more animal instincts, but behaviors we pick up from other people.

We develop a consciousness of ourselves and of what others are doing. We relate all of this in simple ways to the needs we recognize. We use our resources and we use others to meet the needs for food, light, and shelter. This is the beginning of a lifelong process of satisfying our own needs.

Abraham Maslow, a late president of the American Psychological Association, described five sets of human needs that motivate human life. Each set of needs must be met. As the first is met, the person can deal with the second, then the third, and so on. All five of these needs stay with us for life. Although they emerge more or less in the order given here, none is exclusively a childhood need.

1. Physiological (bodily, physical) needs. Early in life it becomes clear that there are needs for food, sleep, and physical activity.

2. Safety needs. As the child begins to move about, his safety and security are sometimes threatened. Then the need for protection from harm and injury emerges.

3. Love and belongingness needs. As we develop a sense of being a person, the needs for acceptance, affection, and social approval grow. What others think becomes very important.

4. Esteem needs. In adolescence and young adulthood, the dominant needs are for self-respect, status, and proof of one's own social adequacy.

5. Self-fulfillment needs. Normal adulthood is not free from needs. But the needs focus on personal growth. Matters of social skills and insights, including a sense of fulfillment, are more important. The adult seeks for reassurance that life has indeed been worthwhile and that he has really made a contribution to others (from *Motivation and Personality*, Harper, 1954).

How does Maslow's list of needs affect the matter of values? Take one set of needs and think about it. Remember that whatever a person finds to meet these needs will be valued.

Where do values come from? The most deeply held values come from the sense of one's needs being met. Where do the needs come from? They are part of being created human.

Spiritual Values

What are *spiritual* values? Maslow's list doesn't deal with this matter, but the similarity isn't hard to see. As a person develops, he or she becomes aware that beyond the physical, social, and personal aspects there is a dimension of life that leans toward the supernatural—toward the mysteries of the universe and the purpose of life itself. The physical world asks and answers the questions of what, who, when, and where, but the *why* of life is still unanswered. A God-consciousness emerges and the person discovers spiritual need. This need too will be met somehow or will be suppressed. Whatever meets the need or whatever suppresses the need will be valued.

For Christians, a personal relationship with Jesus Christ is valued above all else because it meets our most basic spiritual need. For some nonbelievers, the consciousness of spiritual need is met through humanitarian good works. For others it is met by suppressing the need through a sort of worship of human intellect.

Moral Values

For the Christian, as for any religious person, spiritual values and moral values are related. One's Christian experience is surely more than a fire insurance policy against hell. Being born again has eternal meaning, but it has meaning for today too. For one thing, the Christian is confronted with very stringent demands: "I urge you therefore, brethren, by the mercies of God, to present your bodies a living and holy sacrifice, acceptable to God, which is your spiritual service of worship" (Rom. 12:1).

This matter of being a living sacrifice has to do with our value system. It means that our self-centered values need to be brought under God's authority. For the Christian, moral values are the vital outgrowth of religious experience. We become God's partners in a lifelong development project.

Let's look at it one step at a time. First, what are moral values? If tastes are values, investments are values, and ways to meet basic needs are values, what makes a value a *moral* value? Any value that affects the well-being of even one other person is a moral value.

Consider the matter of taste: does your preference for chocolate ice cream adversely affect any human being's welfare? No; so it is not a moral issue. Try another: is hurting someone a moral issue? Yes. Now try these questions: is overeating a matter of moral values? is helping an injured stranger a moral matter? what about ignoring a stranger in church?

The particular lists of "do and don't" matters in any religion fall into two clusters: the ritualistic and the moral. Among the world's religions, Christianity is rather light in the ritualistic and very heavy in the moral. Try this distinction on the following list—Which are ritualistic values and which are moral values?

Not stealing
Not being greedy
Being truthful
Respecting the rights of others
Bowing one's head when praying

As I see it, the first four are matters of moral value, and the last one is a ritualistic value. But on the matter of posture in prayer it's likely that we're talking about a cultural value. This would be no more a moral issue or a biblical matter than whether or not a church building needs a steeple. Taste sometimes sneaks up wearing a "moral" coat. Don't be taken in!

Family

Through family experiences we learn many of the most important values. The family is a strong shaper of values, though rarely as predictable as suggested in the popular phrase "handing down the values from generation to generation."

The value development process is complex. When you understand what's going on, you may be in a better position to do something constructive. In the following chapters we will look at the matter of moral values—what they are, where they come from, how they develop, and how family relationships can play a part.

2

THE FAMILY IS A VALUE

In the animal kingdom some creatures have no sense of family at all. Some animals give birth and that's as far as the family relationship goes. But God created human beings with certain needs that call for a family. The human family provides shelter, protection, care, a sense of belonging, a learning environment, and a secure base from which the grown child is launched into a new family unit.

God's Family
The family is especially important to Christians. God's special relationship with His people is intended to be carried out through families. In the Old Testament, parents were responsible for the spiritual and moral growth of their children. Today's notion that schools or agencies can serve as substitute parents is not based on God's Word.

A Christian family can choose among three ways to view the duty to provide for the children's spiritual and moral development. The first view claims that the family is responsible and should not count on any outsiders to help in the moral and spiritual instruction of the children. This viewpoint is the most conservative, and in many ways the most biblical. It suggests the frontier family living on the edge of civilization. But this choice assumes that the family is a lonely island. It assumes that there are no worthwhile values in the community and little or no likelihood that any social grouping larger than the family can be developed.

The second view holds that the family is inadequate as the source of the children's moral and spiritual development. In our complex society, the family's only hope for moral and spiritual growth is to get lots of help. At the heart of this choice is a need to transfer the family's duty to someone else. This second choice is behind the idea that churches, especially Sunday Schools, should replace the family in matters of the moral and spiritual nurture of children. More often than not, this view is not so much a conscious decision as a willingness to accept agencies, organizations, and institutions as an "easy way out."

The third view is that the family is primarily responsible. Even though help can rightly be sought, the responsibility stays in the family. This third view is a combination of the best features of the other two. It assumes that there is no way to push the responsibility for family development off onto someone else.

Our development takes place over a lifetime. Close relationships with other people are important in the developmental process. It follows, then, that the family is needed to provide key learning experiences—for the children and adults.

Hopeless Holds on Yesterday

Today's family is caught between two forces: the traditions of the self-sufficient, independent family, and the overwhelming trends toward institutionalism.

The past traditions arose as a reaction to the deplorable living conditions from which our European ancestors escaped. (Those who have seen William Hogarth's prints or read Charles Dickens are familiar with the gross injustices which many women and children of England endured in the 18th and 19th centuries.) In the new world, the colonists and frontiersmen pursued the ideal family environment. As the brave patriarch, the father provided for the family by his own resources. Other family members contributed effort and emotional support. Families were large enough to be small, self-sufficient communities.

Some still hold tightly to this dream and thus suffer psychological bruises. They discover that the dream is out of reach. The resulting guilt and anxiety take a terrible toll.

We must accept the fact that we are not frontier pioneers. Ours is not the *Little House on the Prairie.* We live in a complex technological society. A few families can still cut wood for the fireplace, but they probably use a chainsaw produced on an assembly line. Today those who see home-canning, weaving, or candle-making as much more than delightful hobbies are completely unrealistic.

Institutions Invade

Only a generation ago, one parent was at home all the time in most families. But today's cost of living often forces both parents into the working world.

Through all of this, society's institutions have taken over one by one the former duties of the family. Think about it: Whose responsibility is it to care for the elderly? Where do you go when children are born or when someone is seriously ill? Where does the money come from when you are out of work? What happens when your house burns down? There was a time when the family supplied these needs, but not today.

Today when there's a flood, the government moves in with substitute housing. When there's an epidemic, the public health service moves in with vaccines and clinics. When there's no one at home to care for the children, the government moves in to provide day-care centers. And here's where we begin to wake up.

All of this institutionalized care is good news and bad news. It is good news if the only alternative is suffering and neglect. But it is bad news if it *encourages* neglect and laziness. When organized programs remove the sense of personal moral duty, they destroy important values.

In our society, neglect is everywhere—neglect that was rarely seen in simpler days. Easing our consciences by paying more taxes has become the solution. Does my neighbor have a need? Is my neighbor hungry? Thirsty? Sick? Cold? Why worry—we pay taxes to cover these needs.

But here's the problem: If our government didn't provide for these needs, people would suffer. Those who are already needy, especially people who cannot find jobs, would suffer most. On the other hand, as we use massive institutional and government programs to meet these needs, we lose the personal touch. We become less human and more mechanical. What can be done? No one seems to know.

Victims

The family unit is one of the serious casualties in this process of dehumanization. Recently, *Newsweek* reported a variety of troubling observations:

Parents feel increasingly powerless in the face of institutional interference. The growth of social services, health care and public education has robbed them of their traditional roles as job trainers, teachers, nurses and nurturers./And their control over their children's lives is threatened by the pervasive—and increasingly authoritative—influences of television, school and peer groups. "Our oldest daughter is only 7, and already we can see the peer pressure at work. . . . She'll come home and tell us that so-and-so has this and why don't we? . . . I know she needs social exposure, but at the same time we'd like to shelter her from other people's values—like television, easy money, and the idea that you have to go here and go there to have fun."

In their confusion, parents have increasingly turned to experts for advice—and in the process ended up relinquishing more responsibility. . . . "By convincing the housewife and finally even her husband to rely on outside technology and the advice of outside experts, the apparatus of mass education—the successor to the church in our secularized society—has undermined the family's capacity to provide for itself," says University of Rochester historian Christopher Lasch (Kenneth L. Woodward, et al, *Newsweek*, 5/15/78) pp. 64-65, 67.

The secular society has gradually accepted the default of the family. Already a search has begun to find something to replace it. A growing number of children in the United States are raised in single-parent households, (the estimate is now one out of six). Welfare systems and public institutions are expected to care for health, nutrition, protection, and basic learning needs that formerly were a family matter. With a little imagination, we can easily picture public agencies that will be responsible for the child's moral development as well.

Family Farewell?
The traditional family is vanishing. It is dying of neglect and disinterest. Aside from certain unpopular voices among religious and certain secular leaders, few mourn the passing of the stable family.

Today more than half of all mothers of school-age children work outside the home. So do more than a third of the mothers of children under three years old. Of the children born in the 1970s, two out of five will live at least part of their childhood with a divorced or separated parent. At the present rate, only three out of five newly married couples will stay together.

Three Basic Principles. These facts bring us to those crucial values that distinguish the Christian family. Regardless of the particular style or structure of the family, three basics exist: *love, fidelity* (between marriage partners), and *responsibility* (especially for the loving nurture of the children).

Fidelity is at stake today. All of us are victims, to some degree or another, of today's loose sexual standards. The Bible persistently warns against taking sexual matters lightly.

Why such emphasis on sexual standards in the Bible? Because the sexual relationship is part of the family foundation. Responsibility is also at stake. The depersonalized society makes it easy to shirk any sense of duty. Indeed, some words are becoming meaningless—responsibility, duty, obligation. The home where Christian love, fidelity, and responsibility are taught is honoring to God. With this kind of background, biblical concepts are easier to understand. The Bible uses the imagery of *father* to describe God; and *family* terms (sonship, brothers, sisters, born, adopted) to explain relationships among Christians. How can you understand these ideas if you have never experienced them? With no point of reference, these descriptions become abstract concepts.

Many people have never had a warm, loving relationship with their fathers. With such deprived backgrounds, no wonder so many Christians don't grasp the biblical concept of God as our Father.

Variations

The basic principles of the family, like all moral principles, are universal. They are God-given through the creation and are reconfirmed generation after generation from within the nature of humankind. If we believe in basic moral principles, we must also realize the importance of cultural differences. Any particular principle can be fulfilled in various ways, depending on the culture. For example, *family* is a value; the basic principles upon which family is built are three: *fidelity* and *responsibility*, as fulfillments of *love*.

Does this argue for a *nuclear* family (mother, father, and several children) as it has been seen historically in North America? Or does it rather support the idea of an *extended* family (all the aunts, uncles, and grandparents too) so typical in parts of Europe, Asia, and Latin America? Or does this suggest that *tribal* families are somehow unbiblical? No, to all of these questions.

We should respect the different ways important principles are fulfilled. We should not have major arguments over anything less than the basic principles. In matters of family, let's concentrate on the moral principles of love, fidelity, and responsibility. Through these, the family *is* a value.

3

Where Do Good Values Come From?

This book is for Christians. Anyone who loves the Lord Jesus Christ loves God's Word and values God's law. The Christian has a unique way of approaching matters of values. How the Christian determines what is right or wrong is different from the way a secular person does. Even when the Christian comes to the same conclusion as the secular person, he or she likely has taken into account different factors.

View from the Rock
Religious people, in general, are criticized for being too sure of themselves. Maybe it is a fair criticism. Surely someone whose feet are on a rock will slip less than someone whose feet are in mud.

People who seem to have it too easy are often resented. In some ways Christians have it too easy. We have found in Christ the way, the solid foundation, the truth, the real life. It's easy to stop right there, feet on the rock, head in the clouds, and crow about it. What bystanders wouldn't be at least slightly turned off?

Just let a Christian grow in spiritual maturity and the bystander will sing a different tune. At first, the complaint was that the Christian was shallow and trite. Now the onlooker sees a level of spirituality emerging and begins to criticize the Christian's tendency to be aloof and too isolated from the "real world." But when the Christian's spiritual depth develops into a deep burden for God's work of redeeming the world, the critic changes the tune again. He complains (about the mature Christian) that no one has any right to be so confident.

Consider Jesus and His onlookers. Jesus said, "I am the Way, and the Truth, and the Life; no one comes to the Father, but through Me" (John 14:6). Was this any way to make a hit with the crowd? Hardly. But Jesus said it because it was true. Like it or not, the crowd couldn't possibly make sense out of what He said and did unless they faced up to this basic fact.

Overlap. What Christians value based on God's Word overlaps with what morally upright unbelievers value because of traditional social ethics. But there are important differences. In the years to come, these differences are likely to get larger. On one important matter there always has been and always will be an important difference of opinion: *Who says so?* That's the biggest issue.

It began in the Garden of Eden. "Did God say . . . ?" The first three words of the serpent ask, in effect, On whose authority have you decided how you should act? Who says so? It is a very natural question for an unbeliever. Anyone who believes that there is no God, or that we cannot know what God is or what God values, assumes that anything which has been said or written must have a human source. Behind everything is a person or group of persons. So it is always a fair question to ask, "Who says so?" and whenever one doesn't like what has been said, to bring it back to a matter of personal argument: "Who is he (or she) to say? What special right or superior knowledge does he (or she) claim to have?"

Humanism
The secular humanist has come to many of the same conclu-

sions about good and evil as the Christian. Therefore the humanist is likely to challenge the Christian's source. Knowing his or her sources to be human philosophy, personal moral sensitivity, and educated insight, the humanist doesn't see why the Christian would want to claim any different sources. What sort of pompous bigotry would cause a person to claim to have heard from a particular god?

Thus it will always be. How sad that secular humanity, even in its most moral forms, denies the power and the authority that lies behind all goodness (2 Tim. 3:5). Those who do not know God argue for other ways to explain everything. The earth and skies are a reality, not because of God's creative work, but because they originated as the fallout of some cosmic accident. Humankind is the biological marvel of the universe, not because of God's special act of creating us "in His own image," but because of random spontaneous changes, natural selection, and evolution.

Human creations in art, science, and technology do not reflect God's creative nature, but show the result of education. A person's persistent coping with moral matters of truth, justice, and mercy are not because God imparts these concerns. Instead, the humanist believes that we cope with these moral issues because we aspire to goodness through our intellects, our awareness of history, and the evolution of philosophy.

One outcome of this spiritual blindness is the tendency to scoff at lists of virtues. In every age the forces of evil make humanists their unwilling accomplices. Of any statement of the basic difference between good and evil, the humanist asks, "Who says so?" The more blatant forces of evil make this question of doubt the cutting edge of their sword. Thus the humanist finds that human history unsteadily soars into heights of splendor, then plunges into pits of wickedness. People cannot provide their own source of release from this continuous struggle between the values of God and the values of evil. God provides the way, but His statements are challenged and often disregarded. Thus, apart from knowing

Jesus Christ, people—no matter how brilliant—are lost.

Knowing Truth

In our time, especially with the scientific discoveries about the nature of moral judgment, it is becoming less popular to hold to any statements of moral principles. Today, the emphasis is on moral process; moral education helps the structure of moral judgment emerge. But when the matter of moral *truth* is raised, we find how thoroughly the humanists are in command.

Make no mistake about it: the Christian is concerned with both moral judgment as a process and with the *content* of those judgments. It is very important that we see that the Word of God provides moral content. We do not need to search to discover what is good and beautiful. God puts it right on the line.

Three-part platform. God is specific when He provides a platform of moral content. In the Bible, three kinds of material help us see the moral foundation: God's laws, especially in the Old Testament's statements of God's Commandments; moral examples and object lessons, seen in the experiences of people and their dealings with God; and the life and teachings of Jesus Christ and His first followers.

Yes, God provides a platform or foundation; things aren't so wishy-washy as many people would have us believe. But, beyond this, God expects people to reason things out. He expects us to make choices and decisions, to use the moral judgment that is a key feature of being very special creatures.

Once, some people were trying to trap Jesus on a political issue. They asked Him if He thought it right that Jews should pay taxes. The issue was that such taxes were being collected by the occupying Roman government, which was not exactly on the best of terms with the Jewish people. Jesus asked to see the particular coin in which the taxes were to be paid. "Whose picture and name are on this coin?" He asked. "Caesar's," came back the answer. "Well, since Caesar has his marks all over it, it must belong to him. Give Caesar what

belongs to him, and give to God what belongs to God."
(Compare Matt. 22:15-22.)

This sounds simple at first. Then it dawns on you. He put
the responsibility for the judgment right back on the people.
Jesus expects mature people to hear the principle and to act
on it.

Qualities

"Finally, brethren, whatever is true, whatever is honorable,
whatever is right, whatever is pure, whatever is lovely,
whatever is of good repute, if there is any excellence and if
anything worthy of praise, let your mind dwell on these
things" (Phil. 4:8).

Take a close look at these qualities: true, honorable, right
(just), pure, lovely, of good repute (gracious)—what a list!
You may say, "All sweetness and light; big, fat, useless
generalizations." Or you can get serious about it and say,
"God is asking me to look closely and to judge." Is it
truthful? Is it right and pure? If not, it's not honoring to
God.

Is my life honorable, respectable, and respectful? If not,
God won't be pleased. Is it just? God invites each of us to
join in the quest for justice; is there anything more exciting?
Are my actions pure? God's own purity is the measuring
stick; how rarely will we find something to be pure—but it is
nonetheless our concern.

Is my life lovely? Not *lovely* in the superficial sense, but
with the meaning of being crafted with loving hands. God is
worthy of our best for His glory. Is it gracious? Indeed, does
it show the calm and hospitable manner worthy of the
followers of the Prince of Peace?

Those who take the Bible seriously see the importance of
these qualities. They are part of the teachings of our Lord
and of the Apostles. They relate to our lives. Strength of
character, for the Christian, is shaped and determined by the
response we make to these teachings. Do we really want to be
Christlike?

Fruit of the Spirit

The works of God in a person's life are sometimes called the "fruit of the Spirit." These effects provide an interesting list: "But the fruit of the Spirit is love, joy, peace, patience, kindness, goodness, faithfulness, gentleness, self-control; against such things there is no law" (Gal. 5:22-23).

Is there any need to grope around wondering what it means to develop in godliness, as holy saints in the process of redemption? The letters to the Galatians (5—6) and to the Ephesians (4—5) are gold mines for study of the key values of Christian life.

Here are a few of the nuggets of gold:

"Bear one another's burdens, and thus fulfill the law of Christ" (Gal. 6:2).

Note that the "law of Christ" refers to the new commandment that Jesus gave His followers:

"That you love one another, even as I have loved you" (John 13:34). Loving as Jesus loved is not a selfish love; it is a giving, other-centered, burden-bearing love. This is a key value for the Christian.

"Let us not become boastful, challenging one another, envying one another" (Gal. 5:26). The Christlike life makes little room for self-congratulation and seeking after honors. Cutting others down, envying, pride, competing in order to advance oneself at the cost of others—these are things to avoid.

"I . . . entreat you to walk in a manner worthy of the calling with which you have been called, with all humility and gentleness, with patience, showing forbearance to one another in love, being diligent to preserve the unity of the Spirit in the bond of peace" (Eph. 4:1-3). Patience—how demanding a virtue! Patience that gives the road to others. Patience that builds unity and strives for peace. But many of us are selfish. Because of our selfishness, God keeps reminding us that He honors patience—the kind of patience that only He can develop.

This brings up another vital value, the value of forgiveness:

"Let all bitterness and wrath and anger and clamor and slander be put away from you, along with all malice. And be kind to one another, tender-hearted, forgiving each other, just as God in Christ also has forgiven you" (Eph. 4:31-32).

Forgiveness. Nothing is more important in showing Christlike love than a willingness to forgive and the humility to ask for and accept forgiveness. Being a Christian puts a person in the middle of a continuous forgiving situation: since none of us is perfect, God continues to forgive as we confess our sins. In turn, we welcome the occasions in which by forgiving we restore relationships with our family and friends. Indeed, forgiveness too is a key value.

All of these values we call "good" because God does. They are to form the basis of our judgment. God is willing to forgive when our behavior falls short. God wants our judgment to develop, but, meanwhile, our behavior often needs to be forgiven.

As we look further into the matter of moral judgment, bear in mind that God is concerned about more than how well we reason. God is concerned about our moral *action*. And in His Word, moral action is defined quite clearly. The values of Christianity add up to one thing—a person—Jesus Christ, our Lord. Through Jesus Christ we see moral action; through Him we also find forgiveness.

4

God's Law and Christian Values

Talking about rules and law is not popular today. Many people resent the idea that there are certain things they must do and other things they must *not* do. I recall from childhood how often we answered, "Who says so?" "Yeah, you and who else?" "Well, I won't do it because I don't want to." Today it is not only children who talk this way; adults who "do their own thing" are quick to react against rules and regulations. The whole world seems to have become ungovernable and beyond reach of authority, unless the authority uses force—or unless people happen to agree with the rules.

Orderliness
Orderliness is a value. Orderliness comes from a sense of common agreement about standards and rules. Regardless of whether the rules are clearly stated or just a matter of common agreement, orderliness cannot exist without rules. How long does a game last if the players have different ideas about the rules?

Personal responsibility shows itself in orderliness. During the university's registration for dormitory rooms, I saw a sign that read, "If you don't like to keep your room clean, sign up for a different dorm." Another dorm had a similar poster: "If your mother picks up after you, bring her along." Even such a "little" matter as being neat has a lot to do with how well you get along with others.

One reason that orderliness has such a bad name is that some people overemphasize it. When a person gets fussy and pushy about every little thing, whatever that person stands for becomes distasteful. When Christians are crabby about neatness or other minor matters, it puts the whole idea of rules in a bad light.

In recent years, the whole world seems more aware of the danger in blindly following after law and order. We have seen innocent people hurt in the name of law and order. The people who talk the loudest about law and order often turn out to be vicious and lawless. We have even seen moral people picking which laws to obey in terms of personal preferences. (For example, what does it mean when a "clergy" emblem is on a car going 70 miles per hour?) People have learned to be suspicious of law and order.

Unfortunately, these suspicions spill over on God's laws. Is this new? Perhaps it is a deeper tendency than it was a generation ago. But historically, we can see the inclination to overlook or choose against God's way, since the Garden of Eden.

Commandments Within
When Christians refer to God's Law, they usually mean the Ten Commandments (sometimes called the Decalogue). When God gave the Law to Moses on Mount Sinai and carved them in stone, it was not the first time that God's people heard about His moral standards. Many years earlier, Joseph had known that adultery was wrong. Moses had known that it was wrong to kill the Egyptian soldier. When the Law was written down on the tablets of stone, the only thing new was the written record.

God created us and He intended that we should share with Him the awareness of moral responsibility. Because of the way God made us, His Law is embedded in our consciences. In the letter to the Romans, the Apostle Paul said that even those who have never heard of the written law have *within them* the awareness of God's Law (Rom. 1:18-20; 2:14-15).

Every nation and tribe find some way to deal with murder, theft, unfaithfulness, and their awareness that there is a force to be worshiped. These awarenesses are a part of being human. To clarify these matters and to find the universal standard, we turn to God's written Word. Because we can read what God has said, we know what lies at the heart of right and wrong.

Does this clarity help us or hinder us? Because we have before us God's Law are we less free? Would we be better off if we had no basis of moral order?

Two Attitudes
God's Law can be seen in two different ways. Those who resent law see God's Law as a nuisance, or worse, they see it as the reason for their problems. ("Why can't God leave us alone?") Those who know of God's love see God's Law as a generous act of kindness. If God hadn't cared about us, why would He have bothered to point out the basic moral rules of life?

God in His love has given us His moral map to use in the confusing, shifting, slippery twists and turns of life. We can be confident in God's Word. Thus we don't have to try everything to find the harm in it, nor do we have to waste ourselves in moral blindness wondering where we went wrong.

Since there are moral dangers, it is important to know about them. It is sad when a person is so independent that he or she resents being warned of a slippery spot in the trail or a scorpion in a sleeping bag. People who seem determined to hurt themselves resent God's Law, seeing it as a set of restrictions.

Restrictions? Take a good look at the Ten Commandments

and you discover that the direction of the statements is positive. Even those Commandments that say "don't" are really very liberating; they suggest some good thing to *do*. They are worded as *don't* statements because they are important warnings.

Ten Kind Warnings

Christians should dig deeper than the general idea of "Ten Commandments" and think specifically about the personal nature of each of the Ten. Our salvation does not depend on keeping these Ten, but keeping God's Law is a mark of the saved. Our happiness and the quality of life itself will be affected by how we use these statements to bring order into our lives. Considering the dozens of matters that God could have talked about as laws, it is exciting that He narrowed them down to Ten. They must *really* be important.

1. *"I am the Lord your God . . . you shall have no other gods before Me" (Deut. 5:6-7).* Everyone worships something. Sooner or later the god of your life becomes obvious to those around you, even if you are not aware of it. To put the Lord God, Creator of the Universe, first in your life is a marvelous place to start. From this commitment, all other values find their proper place.

For some of us, our natural self-centeredness becomes a god and we worship a mirror. For others, the appetites of greed become a god. These gods enslave; they cannot liberate. The pagan gods of superstitious religion and witchcraft trap people in fear or in false confidence. Just as surely, the gods of selfish wealth and selfish pleasure will enslave those who do not put God in first place.

We can be grateful that God lets us see that the first rule for an orderly life is to put Him in first place. By doing so, we discover that being a servant of the Most High God is a liberating relationship. It liberates us from the false gods that otherwise would make us their slaves.

2. *"You shall not make for yourself an idol . . . you shall not worship them or serve them; for I, the Lord your God,*

am a jealous God, visiting the iniquity of the fathers on the children . . . but showing loving-kindness to thousands, to those who love Me and keep My commandments" (Deut. 5:8-10). The second commandment is a clear warning against idolatry. God warns us that nothing should come between us and Himself. In our culture, idolatry is not a matter of little shrines with stone gods on shelves. But we do have trouble with symbols.

We look around for symbols or emblems to represent our experiences. Consider the apparently harmless matter of collecting stickers from each place you visit on a trip. The valuable experience, the *reality*, is the trip. The sticker or decal is but a symbol to which you attach your memories. So what's the problem? Sooner or later the matter of searching for and buying the stickers becomes the major reason for travel. I have seen people making themselves miserable wasting valuable time looking for those status-symbol stickers. How easily our graven images become outward shows that hinder the *real* experience.

God warns us about this. He intends us to be free from the tendency to let symbols replace reality. He is our Lord in *fact*, not in fantasy. Notice how this commandment ends with a focus on love. God wants to show steadfast love. The reality is the relationship. Wearing a cross to symbolize your relationship with Christ is surely no sin, but God warns that symbols can crowd out the reality.

3. *"You shall not take the name of the Lord your God in vain" (Deut. 5:11).* Here is a commandment that people like to complain about. It's a *don't* statement. You have to think twice to see what might be liberating about it. Notice that it doesn't refer to those less creative forms of swearing that arise from preoccupation with basic biological functions. No, the commandment refers to God's name and it is concerned with a sense of respect and reverence. To be so aware of God's presence that you wouldn't want to be impolite is liberating.

Using God's name—or anyone's name—in vain involves

an offense to the person. Swearing is evil because it attacks the dignity and honor to which God—or a person created in God's image—is entitled.

What happens to your relationship with a friend or family member if you get so careless that you offend that person without even meaning to? How can you be free from harming the relationship? By staying on such close terms that nothing offensive comes between you. This is what God wants. Stay close and you won't be careless about His reality or His name.

4. *"Observe the Sabbath Day, to keep it holy . . . six days you shall labor and do all your work . . . you shall remember that you were a slave in the land of Egypt, and the Lord your God brought you out of there by a mighty hand and by an outstretched arm; therefore the Lord your God commanded you to observe the Sabbath Day" (Deut. 5:12-15).* More silliness has been loaded onto this commandment than any other. Since the earliest years of the church, the day of special meeting and religious observance for Christians has been the *first* day of the week. But never forget, *Sabbath* means seventh; there is no need to change this commandment. Christians hold to the seventh, but put the emphasis on the *first* seventh not the last seventh.

With the exception of a few groups, Christians don't keep the Sabbath. Do we stand before God unrighteous because of this "failure" to "keep Sabbath"? As Jesus pointed out to the Pharisees, lots of issues are more important, "The Sabbath was made for man, and not man for the Sabbath" (Mark 2:27). What does this mean? It means that the Sabbath was a symbol of liberation in itself. How sad that we have let the Sabbath matter become an oppressive burden. The basic principle of the Sabbath deals with respect for the completeness of creation. The finished work of Christ at Calvary also has to do with completeness, but of the *new* creation.

Why was the Sabbath established? Take a good look at the text from Deuteronomy. Notice the word "therefore" in the text. It is a clue that the *why* has just been stated: once you were slaves in Egypt, but now you are free!

So the Sabbath was *not* Israel being humbled into a day of inactivity by God, but was just the opposite: for a people who had been forced to work day in, day out, as slaves, the Sabbath was a great shout of praise that they no longer had to work for others and for an ungodly kingdom, but for themselves and for the kingdom of God. The Sabbath: A great day of happiness, smiles, and family, focused on liberation. God has liberated us from drudgery and from being required to serve the secular system.

Is it different for Christians? It shouldn't be. Yes, we celebrate the first day: Sunday, the first one-seventh of the week. We celebrate liberation at the beginning of the week. Sunday is the double celebration: deliverance *into* a new life in Christ. Our slavery in sin is equivalent to the Jewish experience in Egypt. God led us into His promised land, the kingdom of God. But the parallel ends here.

The new deliverance is not through Moses, but through Christ who sits at the right hand of God the Father. Our celebration is for deliverance *into* the "new week" of life in Christ. The early Christians, with their rapidly developing insights into the principles of the Old Testament, spotted all of this symbolism and shifted their Sabbath Day observance into the first day of the week, the day of new beginnings. The Lord's Day!

The most satisfying and God-honoring way to observe the principle of the Sabbath is to set the one-seventh part of the week apart as a personal, family, and church observance of the celebration of deliverance and liberation. God makes us free. Once a week we need to be reminded that there is more to life than the pressures, the demands, and the drudgery of the normal routine. Show me a Christian who treats the Lord's Day like any other, and I'll show you a tired and frustrated Christian.

5. *"Honor your father and your mother"* (Deut. 5:16). The importance of home and family within the Christian community is underlined in this commandment. It is within

the family that the child first realizes that he or she is a moral decision-maker. The moral environment of the family, particularly the value-choices of the parents, are of great importance to the child's development.

Since every human must take those first steps of discovery to find right and wrong, the relationship with the parents is crucial. The parents, if they are doing as God intended, are providing consistent clues about what is right and what is wrong. The child reaches out, tries things, explores, and gets the clues that are needed. The clues must be reliable.

The earliest awareness of moral conscience is simple: some things are right, some things are wrong. The child's moral sense is thus developed. It is important that the child's relationship with the major sources of those clues (the parents) be filled with respect and love.

Then is this law more concerned with what children ought *to do* or what parents ought *to be*?

God's commandment is to *honor* father and mother. The emphasis here is not obedience (though it is included), but respect. Anyone with power can make others obey. But only an honorable person can expect to be honored.

6. *"You shall not murder" (Deut. 5:17).* Four words, no explanation, but they are important. When Jesus wanted to explain the difference between law and principle, He started with something everyone could understand. He started with this law (Matt. 5:21).

Even people who resent God's list of "Don'ts" seem happy enough about this command. Life itself is violated by killing. No society can endure unless it deals with killing.

The terrorists of our time show that the government that cannot deal with killing is no government at all. That message is heard in the random bombings, senseless shootings, and political kidnappings. Killing is the most powerful form of evil communication.

But is killing ever justified? God told Israel to clear the land of evil through warfare. God authorized executions for certain crimes. Yet God did not use the death penalty on murderers such as Moses and David.

I can turn my other cheek to *my* enemies, as God gives me strength. But can I watch you be tortured and killed without defending you? It's not easy to say. Even God's Law doesn't reduce life to a series of black and white push buttons. We are moral creatures. We must observe. We must participate. We must think.

7. *"You shall not commit adultery" (Deut. 5:18)*. This commandment always seems to get too much or too little attention. People either know so little about it that it seems unimportant to discuss, or they know so much about it that they are afraid to discuss it. Either way, the matter of adultery is not a popular discussion topic.

As a matter of fact, this law isn't nearly as related to sex as it is to the matter of faithfulness and interpersonal integrity. When the Old Testament prophets used illustrations based on adultery, they were always dealing with the relationship of God's people to God Himself.

Adultery, in biblical terms, violates the most basic and essential human relationship: the relationship of husband and wife. God isn't trying to keep us from having fun, nor is He trying to trap us with restrictions. Instead, God is warning that no truly liberated life can be built apart from a sense of moral faithfulness.

The old-fashioned notion of a husband and wife being faithful to each other is still the key to happiness and stability in the home. Without sexual faithfulness, the endless round of suspicions, uncertainties, and sneakiness create such emotional garbage that there is no sense of freedom.

Sexual desires are a fact of life, and Christians are no different from the rest of the human race. We acknowledge our sexuality happily, because God has made us. The sexual experience is the human celebration of love, the ultimate in giving and receiving, the physical renewal of oneness in body and spirit, and the symbol of God's involvement with human beings. But most importantly, it is the emotional bond that holds the husband and wife together as the ups and downs of life bash against the door.

Is sexual experience a value for a Christian? Yes. Sex in its right place is vitally important and a powerful positive value for a Christian. However, outside of marriage it is a negative value—and not because we are against the experience itself. Rather, it is because we are so much for it that we don't want to see it damaged. God's Law points toward liberation. How can a person be truly free while being victimized by the compulsions of his or her animal instincts?

8. *"You shall not steal" (Deut. 5:19)*. One of the earlier experiences of childhood is the experience of ownership: *my* mother, *my* toy, *my* food, *my* bed. Let any of these be "stolen" and the reaction is quick.

As we grow up, this sense of ownership expands. That car (boat, television, stereo) is mine. I bought it; I made it; I earned it; it was given to me. What's mine is mine.

It isn't quite as easy to say, "What's yours is yours." A thread of "grab it" is woven into human nature. Even when we know better, a tendency to reach out and take what isn't ours sometimes slips in.

Every society deals somehow with stealing. But they may not all define it the same way. For example, in parts of Latin America anything left unattended, even a bicycle left outdoors at night, is assumed to mean "I no longer want this. If you need it, help yourself." But in the same situation, a person would be treated to a slashing knife if the bicycle were taken from the *inside* of the house.

Indeed, orderliness in a family and in a nation depends on a clear idea of what is and what isn't right, in matters of property. Is it wrong to exploit others by taking things that are theirs before you are aware of their value? Is it stealing to give a person four quarters for a dollar bill? Hardly. But what if you make the trade knowing that the dollar bill is a collector's item? Christians must face these issues because God's Word teaches that stealing is wrong.

9. *"You shall not bear false witness against your neighbor" (Deut. 5:20)*. The ninth commandment deals with

truth. As God's people, we are to be people of truth. Truth is a basic value in the Christian community. We should even think twice about the little white lies that make things "nice"—half-truths, exaggerations, and insincere compliments. Our commitment to truth should be as complete as the limitations of being mortal will allow. We regard trustworthiness as one of the marks of God being in us.

For Christians, the value of truth is not upheld by saying things that are only technically correct. Bearing false witness suggests that one is telling something untrue about another. But it also covers two other kinds of untruthfulness.

What about silent withholding of the truth? If a judge asks, "Did anyone see this man on the night of August 12?" and you did and don't speak up, you may not have told a lie, but you have been a false witness.

Consider also the matter of half-truths. What if a judge or another person in the court asks, "Did you see this man steal the necklace?" Since you didn't actually see him take it out of the drawer you say, "No, I didn't." You know that before he went into the bedroom he didn't have it and when he came out he did. Is it right to hide behind the fact that you gave a technically correct answer? You have made a false witness, because for the Christian, a statement is untruthful if it is misleading. The issue is more than the lie; it is false witness.

What would happen if we were constantly deceiving each other? If you couldn't count on what anybody said and you knew nobody believed you either, would you feel very free? Of course not. Is God's Law a burden? No, once again it points to the liberation that comes from orderliness.

10. "You shall not covet your neighbor's wife, and you shall not desire your neighbor's house, his field or his manservant, his ox or his donkey or anything that belongs to your neighbor" (Deut. 5:21). God's Law separates covetousness (desiring what doesn't belong to me) from stealing. Earlier we saw the law against stealing. Here the emphasis is on that innocent backyard sport of wishing I had my neighbor's boat. I'd never think of stealing it, but what's the harm in dreaming about it?

In Colossians 3:5, the Apostle Paul put coveting together with greediness and called it all idolatry. The Ten Commandments end with a reminder that when *things* become our god, our relationship with God is damaged. Then other relationships begin to suffer.

Jesus urged His followers to guard themselves against covetousness—He called it an uncontrolled desire for wealth and a greedy longing to have more. A man's life does not consist in the abundance of his possessions (cf. Luke 12:15).

On this subject Jesus told the parable of the farmer who became so rich that he tore down his storage bins to build larger and larger. Suddenly he was dead. Who would all this grain belong to now? Such a greedy farmer is a person "who lays up treasure for himself, and is not rich toward God" (Luke 12:21).

The frenzied grasping for things is a trap. God warns that such is the road to enslavement in materialism. Choose instead the liberation of God-centered and people-focused humanity. The Law of God is aimed at building and keeping the integrity of people.

Under the Law?

The Apostle Paul had been educated in a very legalistic tradition. Before becoming a Christian he was a highly respected Pharisee. As a Christian, he knew that God's Law was valuable and good. Yet he saw how useless it was to build a legal road to God.

Paul's answer to the matter of Law had two parts. First, Paul said that a person could stand before God's judgment either as a proud keeper of the Law or as a humble sinner claiming God's grace. If one attempted to stand in selfrighteous pride, all the little flaws would show, no matter how good the behavior had been. The other way to stand, in humility claiming only Christ's righteousness, would be the only way to expect God's grace. For every person who comes to God through the blood of Jesus Christ, the voice of true

Christianity is consistent: "He saved us, not on the basis of deeds which we have done in righteousness, but according to His mercy, by the washing of regeneration and renewing by the Holy Spirit, whom He poured out upon us richly through Jesus Christ our Saviour" (Titus 3:5-6).

Schoolmaster. What, then, is the value of the Law? Paul said that the Law is like a schoolteacher (Gal. 3:24-25). It teaches us that God is a moral God and is very concerned about matters of good and evil. We must make moral decisions in life. God, through the Law, has given us a solid foundation that relates to life's crucial moral choices.

To cover all the issues and decisions about right and wrong would require thousands of laws. The Pharisees had made a good start on creating such a list. They had a law for everything they could think of. They stubbornly insisted that everything in life be viewed as a matter of law. It is no wonder that the Pharisees were so displeased with Jesus. He said that He had come to fulfill the Law, yet it was obvious that Jesus didn't approve of the Pharisees' emphasis on laws.

Jesus was in a difficult situation. On the one hand, the laws of the Pharisees were based on God's laws; their legal furniture was stacked deep, all over the foundation of the Ten Commandments. Jesus had no wish to violate God's Law. On the other hand, the Pharisees were so far from the personal reality of God that they lacked the basic will to please God. As all human beings, they could not keep God's Law. Their guilt was obvious. They wanted others to do what they, themselves, were unable to do—to please God by obeying laws. Jesus called these Pharisees white-washed crocks of decaying bones.

Living by Principles

Jesus did not see the Law of God as a list of rules and regulations. He saw it as principles. He emphasized the two great principles that are basic. The whole Law of God and the teachings of the prophets—the whole Old Testament—make sense because of these two principles, Jesus said.

Taking a look at the religious legalism of His time, Jesus referred to one of these principles as "a new law." In all of their emphasis on law, the Pharisees had missed the crucial principle; Jesus offered it as something they might add to their list. He knew very well it would stand out as being different. It was more than a law, it was the principle of love! "A new commandment I give to you, that you also love one another" (John 13:34).

On another occasion He put both of the basic principles together: The first, He said, was already right in front of their noses as the first of the Ten Commandments: "You shall love the Lord your God with all your heart" (Matt. 22:37). The second principle, He said, was like the first, not lesser nor greater, not separable, not from some different source, but of the same value: "You shall love your neighbor as yourself" (Matt. 22:39).

Here is the important answer to the Pharisees' suspicious question: What did Jesus mean when He said, "I did not come to abolish, but to fulfill [the Law]"? (Matt. 5:17) He meant that instead of either discarding or emphasizing the Law, He came to draw attention to the underlying principles: love between God and human beings and love of people for each other. In these two, all the Law and the prophets hold together (compare Matt. 7:12 and 22:40).

5

How Children See Right and Wrong

I have had playmates, I have had companions,
In my days of childhood, in my joyful school days,—
All, all are gone; the old familiar faces.
> Charles Lamb: *The Old Familiar Faces*

Even with the sentimental memories of happy times, most of us can remember bits and pieces of the other side of the story. The dog that bit, the bloody nose brought on by a difference of opinion about whose turn at bat, the feeling that over and over again we had disappointed those we wanted most to please; and, underlining it all, so many things we didn't understand.

Feelings
Children are rarely as snugly at peace with the world as poets suggest. Frightening mysteries abound—glimpses of adults at war with each other over things that don't make sense, unclear meanings, expectations that can't be met. New things are happening all the time, and even when people listen to a child, many don't understand. If adults don't understand children, then surely children don't understand adults.

Out of this confusion, a sense of right and wrong somehow

emerges. To know what is right and what is wrong is part of the survival need of the child. It is no surprise that the notion of right and wrong has its first meaning for a child in self-centered terms. The child *feels* right and wrong. Only later does the child *know* right and wrong.

Limitations. Being a child has its limitations. Development is a matter of losing these limitations—getting beyond them through the unfolding and the use of more adult forms of reasoning. "When I was a child, I used to speak as a child, think as a child, reason as a child; when I became a man, I did away with childish things" (1 Cor. 13:11).

What does it mean to think as a child? To reason as a child? It's not so much a lack of knowledge but a narrow viewpoint and a limited reasoning process. A child cannot think as an adult. Parents need to realize that a change in reasoning ability comes with maturation. Let's look at a child's view of life and his reasoning processes.

CHILD'S VIEW	CHILD'S REASONING
Self-centered universe	What matters most is me.
Self-satisfying values	What is important is how it affects me.
Sees others as "things"	What is good for me is good for everybody.
Hears moral instruction only as commands	I must keep testing the limits to find out what the rules are.
Sees morality as being determined by rewards and punishments	Whatever it is, it's okay if you gon't get caught.

The development of moral judgment is more complex than physical or mental development. Moral judgment is not something that simply unfolds when fed, nor is it something that can be learned like facts of history. Moral judgment develops through a relationship between what the child discovers about right and wrong (as determined by others in the environment) and what the child discovers about himself or herself as a person.

More Than Environment

Environment doesn't account for everything. Two children can grow up side by side, having virtually the same experiences and engaging in the same relationships, only to turn out as two very different adults. What each child takes into account is different. In making these early connections between outside circumstances and personal feelings, the child shows a great deal of his personality. What one child is sensitive to or aware of, another child will ignore. This difference reflects the inherited factors of personality.

Parents set patterns or models for their children's moral judgments, but each child builds his or her own structure of moral judgment. Parents can't pass it down. The parents' example does not produce moral conscience in the child. Children copy parents' behaviors—at least to see how satisfying the actions may be. A child is apt to talk and act like the parents, whether or not the child believes in what he or she is saying and doing.

Frequent talking with and listening to a child has a valuable effect on moral development. Helping the child think and talk about intentions and consequences of his or her actions is important, especially when the emphasis is on the needs of others. A relationship of contract can be built between parents and child in which the child is "bargained" into meeting standards within his or her skills and abilities. This relationship, if based on respect and fairness, is useful even in dealing with more serious misbehaviors of children and adolescents.

Facing the Facts

In the early 1920s, one of the first modern studies of moral education was conducted at Columbia University by Hugh Hartshorne and Mark May. Their research findings are disturbing even today, especially since they found so little effect from "character education" programs of schools and churches. The research focused primarily on academic cheating and other forms of dishonesty. Hartshorne and May found that people can't be classified as honest or dishonest in any clear-cut way; almost everyone cheats in one way or another some of the time. They also found that dishonesty depends on the situation; a person will cheat in one situation but not in another. Among the most important findings are these two:

1. *What people say about their moral values has little to do with how they act.* This conclusion reminds us that verbal morality is almost useless. If the major goal of our moral teaching is to get children to say the right answers, we are deceiving ourselves. There's a big step from what a person says to what a person does.

2. *The tendency to be honest or dishonest varies according to the situation.* Risk of detention, pressure of the "need to cheat" and the need for group approval are important in making a decision.

Parents should not be surprised at slips in a child's moral actions any more than they are with their own behavior. Parents should consider the degree of temptation that the child can handle. For example, the temptation to play with a pretty vase may be too great for a three-year-old, even if the child is aware of the wrongness of handling it. It's better to move the vase to a higher shelf. But don't count on the higher shelf as a long-term solution. The temptations mount far beyond any parent's ability to shield the child. Within a few years, the whole world will be available.

Power of Peers. Group approval is also a very powerful force—for good and for bad. Group approval is what makes the child want to conform to a particular behavior. When everyone frowns at you, pretty soon you decide not to burp. But if everyone laughs when you burp, you try to do it more often. (Are you visualizing a four-year-old at the dining table, or a half-sober man at a bar? Group approval is the shaping force in either situation.)

Mental Development

Much of what we know about the process of mental development has come from the studies of Jean Piaget (pronounced: Zhahn Pee-ah-ZHAY). This remarkable Swiss psychologist has spent his whole life studying children. His major interest has been in how children think. He has used one of the basic methods of social science: watching.

In his home city, Geneva, Piaget has observed children in all sorts of situations—at play, at school, at home. He has listened closely to how children talk to each other, how they talk to adults, and even how they talk to themselves.

Piaget tells us that a child must be seen as a child. The child is not a miniature adult. A child thinks differently than an adult. A normal adult has developed mental processes that are not available to a child.

A small child is unable to see things from any point of view but his or her own. A lack of intelligence is not the issue; the child simply is locked into one viewpoint or perspective. Because of this, a child has trouble being concerned about other people's feelings.

When an adult does or says something that hurts someone's feelings, we can be sure that either the act is intentional or that the adult is careless. We would likely say that the adult is cruel or insensitive. On the other hand, when a seven-year-old does or says something that hurts our feelings, we should not interpret it as cruel or insensitive behavior. Indeed it may hurt, but the child cares about his own feelings —not someone else's. (Sometimes adults still act like children in this respect, but it's usually because they choose to think in self-centered ways.)

Since the child lacks perspective, should parents try to do something about it? Piaget's research shows that whatever you do, whatever you say, and no matter how you push, the child still has a child's view of life.

In other words, viewpoint is not a matter of information alone. Surely you can teach the child facts. But far more important, you can show him or her that there are other viewpoints. The child can't use facts to reason with until he can mentally transport himself into someone else's shoes. And this sort of maturity takes time.

What sort of understanding would the child have of such an idea as the Golden Rule, "Do unto others what you would have them do unto you"? This distinction between self and others is not made in the reasoning processes of the preschooler. Thus the text will have very limited meaning; more than likely it will get turned around to the simpler idea that if someone does something to hurt me I should hurt that person in return. The child is clear enough about what he or she wants from others, but connecting that idea to the need to do good for others is too much.

Self-centered. Children, especially younger children, are limited to seeing a moral world in self-centered terms. Good is what feels good or works out to one's own advantage. Bad is what feels bad or works out to one's hurt. The distinction between right and wrong is largely limited to these simple notions of personal feeling. Parents ordinarily start early to say, "Bobby, that's a no-no." "Arlie, that's not nice . . . not right . . . we don't do that . . . that's bad." And on it goes, with little effect in leading to moral understanding, but still very necessary—at least to develop the basic vocabulary of moral communication.

The child must learn to associate these words (no, not nice, bad, wrong, and don't) with some sort of *real* or concrete result of having done the thing. Since the child's mind focuses on the concrete, the words have little meaning and no effect until they are attached predictably to a negative or hurtful outcome. This relation must be made in the child's own mind, and it can't be made *for* him or her, no matter how much the parent may try.

Consistency

Moral conscience begins to emerge through the child's own experiences. Few things are more important in a child's early development than having people around who are consistent.

Too much inconsistency is likely to retard the child's moral development. So long as the parent is gentle, almost anything done consistently to help the child find the difference between good and bad behavior will be useful. There are few magic formulas for bringing up children—but being as consistent as possible is perhaps the closest.

Discovery. The child finds the difference between right and wrong. Yes, surely the child has been told the difference; but that is only one part of the process. The learning occurs when the child sees in his or her own actions the possibility of predicting good and bad effects.

Even a small child will begin to look around sheepishly just before or after doing a "no-no." Some children may *do* the wrong action while *saying* the right choice. A little girl may invade the refrigerator and eat something while saying "no-no." The child knows the *no* but is not strong enough to resist temptation. In such a moment you can see the first traces of moral conscience. It is marvelous to watch, and often humorous. But when adults laugh about the child's little "badness," the child becomes confused and is likely to be set back. Too much of this scold-one-time-and-laugh-the-next, and you will have a morally underdeveloped child on your hands.

One other word of caution: the child is not a puppy to be trained. God has created us with a remarkable moral sensitivity. A steady schedule of rewards and punishments isn't needed to awaken it. Gentle, loving consistency is enough; that's the human way.

6

Knowing What You Value and Why

Have you ever taken a good look at your moral values? You know that some things are right and other things are wrong. You pay attention to these values as you go through your day. But have you ever taken a close look? For example, did you ever write a list of things you believe are righteous? Beyond this, do you have any idea why you believe these things are important? What are the deep roots of your view of good and evil? Perhaps the next few chapters will help you get better acquainted with yourself.

The concern for values, especially moral values and ethics, is as old as mankind. In every era of human history, laws, rules, ethical codes, and other concerns with moral behavior have been talked about, debated, and passed down through oral tradition. In literate societies, statements of moral values are among the earliest writings. No evidences of God's use of written records are seen until the time of Moses. At Mount Sinai God inscribed the Law on panels of stone. Thus began Moses' great task of writing down the history of God's people.

Moses is recognized both as the lawgiver and as the author of the Pentateuch. Under the inspiration of the Holy Spirit of God, he wrote down all of the vital experiences from the

Garden of Eden until the entry of the Children of Israel into the Promised Land.

Moral Concerns

The writings of the great philosophers have focused on moral issues and the problem of determining what is good. The ethicists and moralists of all traditions are, as a whole, concerned with matters of good and evil, right and wrong. But all of these studies emphasize the *content* of moral judgment. Placing exclusive emphasis on content tends toward several dangerous oversimplifications:

1. Assuming that being moral is a matter of knowing what is right;

2. Assuming that developing moral judgment is a matter of learning the rules;

3. Assuming that people can be schooled into higher moral standards.

If we make these three errors we might buy into almost any scheme that would give people the right moral answers and then punish them for disobedience. Whenever I hear someone say, "But I told you not to!" I am reminded that being told is not enough. When I say to myself, "I knew better than to do that," I am reminded that knowing is not enough. Indeed, when I think of the patience God shows as He instructs, forgives, corrects, and encourages us, I realize that knowing what God has said is only one small part of being a moral person.

New Emphasis

In recent years a great increase of attention has been given to the *structure* of moral judgment. Many research studies have been made, and our understanding of moral judgment and how it develops has been expanded.

The favorite research procedure for these studies is interviewing. Those who think of scientists as people in white coats who hold smoking test tubes and stopwatches may have a hard time with this fact. Social scientists spend most of their time listening to people.

The newer research is concerned not only with what people believe but with why they believe it. (Don't be too critical of this shifted emphasis; no one is suggesting that *what* you believe is unimportant!) If you have an understanding of the structure of moral judgment, you are better able to help people with the difficult task of decisively acting on what they believe.

Looking for Reasons
It's wrong to steal. Why? It's wrong to hurt people. Why? It's good to love people. Why? It's good to do what Jesus tells us. Why?

Does this sound like a conversation between a small boy and his mother? Perhaps. It could also be a conversation between you and me. I would have asked first, "What things do you think of as *wrong*, and what things do you think of as *good*?" Then, no matter what your answers, one by one, I would have asked, "Why?" In this way you would be a participant in some of the most interesting research of the last decade. In many places in the world (in the United States, England, and Canada, particularly), social scientists have been asking these questions: What do you value? Why do you value it? Why are certain kinds of behavior called *good* while others are labeled *bad*?

The research scientists have been more interested in the Why than in the What. The reason is plain. So much more of the attention of moral philosophers and religious writers has been given to the content of moral issues. Now the rest of the matter is being opened up.

When people grow up, they mature in many ways. Growing up involves changes in one's moral judgment. Most people would recall, however, that since their earliest memories they have known it is right or wrong to do certain things. Does this mean that there has been little development? No, it means that two kinds of change are involved in moral development.

Content

Consider first the content of a moral value. This one is easiest to identify because it is what most people mean when they refer to moral development. What one believes to be right and wrong is the *content* of one's value system.

Why the concern here for the technical vocabulary? Because with this basic distinction between two aspects of moral judgment you see more about what moral development is. You understand better your own experience as a valuing person. Also, you understand what is going on when a person develops morally.

Structure

You need only to be able to make the distinction between content and structure. Try to remember it this way: content is the What of a moral judgment; structure is the Why of a moral judgment.

When you say, "Stealing is wrong," you likely have some reason for saying so. Sometimes these reasons are called beliefs. They may or may not relate to religious beliefs. Scientists call these reasons *structure*.

The structure of a moral judgment is the Why that causes you to hold to the content of the judgment. What you believe to be right or wrong is the content. Why you believe it to be right or wrong is the structure.

Think of the structure of a belief as the framework under a bridge. The surface of the bridge carries the load of the traffic. Underneath is what makes it hold firm—the structure.

When I was a boy, a railroad ran across the end of a lake near where we lived. It was such fun standing at the shore of that lake watching the trains pass high above. They rattled and shook the track, the wooden trestle and, it seemed, the whole earth.

Then World War II started and the railroad was regarded as an important target for sabotage. We watched sadly as day after day carloads of gravel and dirt were dumped through and around the trestle to make a solid pile of earth under the tracks. The old structure was replaced by a new one. The track stayed the same, and the railroad service was not disrupted during the change.

What happens in moral development is much like that. The development of structure may mean a complete change of what lies underneath a moral value, but becoming mature requires the change. The old structure was part of childhood. The new structure reflects the more thorough thought and understanding that mental and social growth bring.

At one level of development a person might be structurally guided by what others will say or expect. At another level of development the person's structure may be dominated by a commitment to the orderliness that rules and laws bring about. Very likely the content of the person's values hasn't changed much during this time. For example, the person may still hold exactly the same position about the wrongness of lying, stealing, cheating, or whatever. The difference is that he or she has a new way of thinking about the moral wrongness and a new mental process to use in making judgments.

Earlier, this person was thinking, "It's wrong to steal because the people who are important in my life will be disappointed or displeased if I steal." Later, the person's thoughts might be: "It's wrong to steal because there are rules and laws against stealing. If I break these laws I won't be doing my part to create the kind of orderly world I want to live in."

Consider the matter of obeying God. Even a small child can learn what God wants him or her to do. Why would the child want to obey God? God is our heavenly Father and He does good things for His children. Or, God is powerful and dangerous; He punishes those who disobey Him. Indeed, both of these ideas are biblical and both are understandable even to small children. So which will it be?

Those who influence the child will determine which emphasis the child will see most clearly, and the child's structure of belief about obeying God begins to form. "I want to obey God because He is my heavenly Father; I want Him to do good things for me." Or, "I want to obey God because He will punish me if I don't." What a difference in structure! At any level of development there are varieties of structure. We are not all alike. Even on the matters of content that we agree on, we might disagree about why we agree.

Moral Judgment

Moral judgment is the mental process by which we decide that a given thing is good or evil. To review the process, read the following interview that illustrates the content and structure of a moral decision.

Q. Did you cheat on the math test this morning?

A. No.

Q. Why not?

A. It is wrong.

Q. What does someone do when he or she cheats on a test?

A. Copy. Or look up the answers. Maybe get someone to help you.

Q. Is that wrong?

A. Yes, on a test it is.

Q. How do you know it's wrong?

A. The teacher said not to.

Q. Is that important?

A. Yes.

Q. Why?

A. Because the teacher makes the rules.

Q. Would it be all right to cheat on the test if the teacher didn't mention it?

A. No.

Q. Why not?

A. Cheating is always wrong.

Q. What is cheating?

A. When you do things dishonestly. When you take credit for things you really didn't do.

Q. What other words can you use for cheating?

A. You could say it's dishonest. Maybe like stealing.

Q. In what way is it like stealing or dishonest?

A. People who cheat steal good grades. That's not honest.

Q. Why is that wrong?
A. You get in trouble when you're dishonest.
Q. What do you mean?
A. Your mother or somebody will punish you.
Q. Are you ever dishonest?
A. Sometimes.
Q. How does that make you feel?
A. It makes me afraid. I don't like it.
Q. Why not?
A. I don't like to get punished.

Notice how the interview goes back and forth between What questions and Why questions, going deeper and deeper into the structure that lies behind the content that cheating is wrong. The first hint of moral structure is found in these words: "The teacher said not to." The interview continues, but the farther it goes the clearer it is that this person thinks of cheating this way:

Content: Cheating is wrong. It is a form of stealing. It is not honest.

Structure: Cheating is wrong because you are likely to be punished for it. The teacher (or possibly another person in authority) determines the rightness or wrongness of the act and has the responsibility to punish violations.

Thinking about how you would have responded to the interview questions would be useful before you read the next chapter. Looking at the what and why of your own values is an important experience. When you have learned to think about both content and structure, you are better able to understand the process of moral judgment.

7

The Development of *Why*

In what ways do people grow up? Physically, they get larger, change in appearance, get stronger and become much more able to use the body in athletic and expressive ways. Sexual characteristics and capabilities emerge, all in a rather predictable sequence.

Emotionally, people get more complex as they grow up. Sensitivities and awarenesses are developed. The capability of response to a wider array of emotional situations emerges. People develop unique personalities, largely a reflection of the complex variety of their emotional characteristics. Emotional maturity suggests the capability of coping with life. The older one gets the more one is exposed to difficult emotional challenges. Being young and dependent provides an emotional shield. Becoming older—growing up—tears away this shield and one must deal with more demanding pressures.

When the responsibilities of parenthood are added, the tests become severe. Being able to handle the emotional problems of adulthood is becoming more a matter in which people need help. In this difficult era, growing up emotionally is harder than ever.

Social Development
Socially, growing up is a matter of accepting the increasing

responsibilities of relationships with other people. Small children can't play together very long without hitting each other. Older children tend to hurt each other with words. Their social relationships need to be supervised.

Growing up socially means going through more or less predictable stages. First one gains an awareness that other people are real and that they too have feelings and a sense of property. Following this is a series of skill development tasks in which the person finds ways to enhance his or her own pleasure and security by relating in certain ways to others. Then comes a more genuine concern for the well-being of others and the development of the skills of kindness.

Mental Development
Mental development is closely related to all these other kinds of development. A person's mental capabilities emerge in a predictable sequence. Not everyone develops at the same rate, but almost everyone moves through the same stages. Jean Piaget has identified the mental development stages as follows:

The *Sensorimotor Stage* begins at birth (some say before). The child begins life with a great deal of dependence on simple senses. Most of the clues the infant gets about the environment come from hitting, kicking, or bumping into things. This rather pitiful and limited way of learning is one of the distinctive features of being human. Most behavior is very simple reaction—a sudden noise might cause a jerking reaction followed by crying; closeness of mother or a bottle of warm milk might start the sucking noises. But whatever learning is taking place is very simple. It might be better explained as getting ready to learn.

In the *Preoperational Stage*, the child still cannot use the mind for any deliberate thinking. Only in very simple ways does the child think at this stage. Thoughts are limited to the child's own experience. Although language skills are developing rapidly in this period, only one idea can be thought of at a time, and the relationship between cause and effect is beyond understanding.

Next is the *Concrete Operational Stage.* In this stage of development, children (and adults too, because not everyone goes significantly beyond this stage) develop useful, logical ways to relate to things and to people. One learns to identify, analyze, and categorize. Telling the difference between a robin and a bluejay is no problem at all. How to put oneself to work, how to convert labor into money, and how to convert money into material possessions are easy uses of the mind in this stage.

The highest stage of mental development is what Piaget calls the *Formal Operational Stage.* When the person has reached this stage, the mind can be used as a formal logic-processing device. In other words, no matter how abstract the idea, the mind can grasp it and "operate" on it. Such abstract questions as "Who am I?" "What is the purpose of life?" "What is truth?" demand formal operations. (From *The Origins of Intelligence in Children*, International Universities Press, 1952.)

Moral development and mental development are not the same; but until a person's mental development has moved forward, moral development will not proceed either. As we will see in the next chapter, moral development and mental development both require some of the same learning experiences.

Three Interviews
To review the stages of mental development, the following chart shows some of the questions and answers that reveal the differences in the way people think at each stage.

I hesitate to put ages on this list because people are different and develop at different rates. The minute parents see an age specified, they check to see if their child is "normal," or, better yet, "ahead of normal." Fretting about what to do to make kids fit the pattern is actually dangerous.

From the list, you can see the shifts that occur from stage to stage. As a matter of fact, this list represents the same boy (now a young man) at three different times in his life. From

RESPONSES ILLUSTRATING THE THREE UPPER STAGES OF MENTAL DEVELOPMENT

Interview Questions	Stage 2: Pre-Operational	Stage 3: Concrete Operations	Stage 4: Formal Operations
Who are you?	Billy	William H. Smith, Junior.	I'm still trying to find out!
Where do you live?	In a house	In Dalton, Georgia.	I live *anywhere*, friend.
Do you sing?	Sure—want to hear me? Lah, Lah, Lee, Lah, Lah	Do I sing what?	Yes, (or No.)
Who is your daddy? (or father)	Him. (pointing)	Mr. Smith.	In what sense?
Are you a "doubting Thomas"?	What?	No.	Sometimes
What's the most important day in your life?	Christmas	My birthday.	The day when I found . . . (or, discovered, began to see . . ., or, entered a particular relationship).
Is friendship important to you?	Yep . . . what?	At least with Bobby and Joe, maybe Arlene too.	Oh, yes, very important.
Where can you learn about the purpose of life?	What?	In books.	Each person must find it for himself.
What is truth?	Not telling a lie	Telling what is right.	It's hard to define, but truth is a sort of principle you believe in.

your own experiences with children, can you estimate his age at the time of the first two interviews? One hint: Bill (not his real name) was 20 at the time of the last interview.

The differences between Stages 2 and 3 are much less important to the matter of values and moral judgment than the contrast between Stages 3 and 4. Although some of the responses in the Stage 4 column aren't particularly precise, we can see that Bill is now thinking about issues. Nothing is quite so black and white anymore. This ability to deal with abstract concepts is necessary for the higher forms of moral judgment. But how does all of this relate to moral development?

Moral Development

An interesting series of research studies has been going on under the direction of Lawrence Kohlberg of Harvard University. Taking his inspiration from Piaget's search for stages of intellectual development, Kohlberg has been looking for evidence of a pattern in moral development. He has found a small amount of predictable change in the content of moral development. But what little evidence there is for predictable changes in moral content is overshadowed by strong evidence that structure of moral judgment develops in predictable patterns.

Kohlberg's own view of the meaning of his findings is still developing. But one conclusion has not changed; moral judgment emerges through three distinct levels. The three levels of moral judgment are most important. Knowing about them helps us to understand ourselves better. They give us a much clearer idea of what the educational and parental tasks really are.

For the Christian, there is a special encouragement in what Kohlberg has found. His research agrees remarkably well with what the Bible teaches about childhood, about unredeemed man, and about moral and spiritual development. However, since he does not claim any Christian beliefs for himself, the way Kohlberg deals with a person's relationship to *authority*, the question of *obedience*, and the *source* of moral good differs from what many Christians believe. Nonetheless, we can be thankful that the research frontier has been expanded. The new insights are helpful for Christians. Kohlberg found that three different kinds of structure account for virtually all moral judgments. (From "Development of Moral Character and Moral Ideology," *Review of Child Development Research*, Vol. 1, Russell Sage Foundation, 1964).

Level I, or preconventional judgment, focuses on me and my concerns. "Good" is what serves my purposes and makes me feel good about it. "Bad" or "wrong" is what hurts me or my own interests. Punishment and reward are the major influences toward moral good. Billy: "I know it's wrong because every time I do it, I get in trouble."

Level II, or conventional judgment, focuses on others. Moral judgments are made on the basis of concerns outside oneself. Early in this level, the way to determine right and wrong depends on what pleases or displeases the people who are important to me. Later in this level, I realize that rules and regulations are the highest form of clear statements about right and wrong. Examples and rules are the major influences toward moral good. Billy: "I don't do that because Jesus wouldn't do it."

Level III, or postconventional judgment, focuses on principles. Moral judgments are made on the basis of principles, especially the principles that underlie the behavior I value in myself and others. Billy: "I don't even want to do that because it wouldn't be consistent with what God is doing within me."

Everyone starts in the first level. As the child begins to have a moral awareness (conscience) and to make moral judgments, the first level is always the one that accounts for the judgment process.

Then as moral judgment develops, we pass from the first to the second structure and then to the third structure. The order is a predictable sequence. (You can still make judgments of the first level sort, but development may have released you into one of the more mature levels.)

But not everyone moves from level to level. Many people stay in the first level. Some adults still use first level moral judgment. Even more people remain in the second level. The second level is especially comfortable if you crave order and accept authority. You might even be happy to remain there. But if you can't accept order and authority, you might go through life in Level I with only yourself as guide.

As we move into higher levels of moral judgment, we do not forget how to make decisions on the simpler level. Instead, we add the new structure to the possible ways of looking at a moral issue. Remember the illustration of the new structure of dirt and gravel for the timber railroad trestle? The new structure became the dominant one, but the old structure was still there, deep inside.

Kohlberg found that at any level, a person can understand moral messages that are tuned to his or her level and that appeal to the structure of that level. When you hear a moral message that is over your head, do you try to bring it down to your level? If so, you may be distorting it.

Kohlberg also discovered that religious conversion has a minimal effect on one's moral judgment. This point causes some Christians to wave the red flag. Surely one's religious experience has some positive effect on moral judgment. But where in the Bible are we promised instant maturity?

Our relationship to God and God's view of us changes promptly through religious conversion. God begins a good work in us (Phil. 1:6). That work of the Holy Spirit is a long and steady process that takes a lifetime. This process is a matter of cooperation with our own will to work with God (Phil. 2:12-13). If it were a matter of instant maturity, why did Peter so emphasize growing? (1 Peter 2:1-3 and 2 Peter 3:17-18)

We need to remember what conversion does and doesn't do. Who among us no longer sins? Who among us claims always to do what is right? Who has completed the moral development process and can smoothly glide through life? "The old things passed away, behold, new things have come" (2 Cor. 5:17). But we are still involved in a day to day growth process. We must keep on laying aside "every encumbrance and the sin which so easily entangles us, and . . . run with endurance the race that is set before us" (Heb. 12:1).

In his research, Kohlberg deals mainly with moral judgment; he is only slightly concerned about moral action. God is concerned primarily with moral action (obedience) and, therefore, He is also concerned with moral judgment. The Christian is concerned with both moral judgment and moral action. A moral act has moral consequences and depends on moral judgment. Our moral actions can be no better than our moral judgments.

Consider the difference between principles and rules. Rules are external. They are the voices of others—of society, of my nation, of God. But principles are internal. I can't bring rules in, they belong to the outside, but I can bring principles in. Principles are what I have selected and brought in from what I respect and value. If God's Law means rules and regulations, it is outside me. But if God's Law means principles, it can come inside and transform me.

Biblical Parallels
Many Christians are suspicious at first. Why does Kohlberg think that the third level is better than the second? Isn't Level II where a Christian ought to be? After all, since righteousness is from God, isn't it external to the human being? Doesn't Level II best represent what God really wants—obedience to His Word and His Law?

Obedience is important, but it is not enough. God wants His people to be changed on the *inside*. God prefers that His Law be written inside on the heart rather than just inscribed on tablets of stone (2 Cor. 3:3). This contrast suggests the distinction between responding to the external Law and changing inside by building one's life on internal moral convictions.

Jesus did not come to destroy the Law, but to fulfill it (Matt. 5:17). In fulfilling the Law, He respected it. But He also demonstrated the two principles that underlie all of God's Laws: love for God and love for other people. The Law is a tutor that brings us to Christ (Gal. 3:24). The Law can't live within us, but Christ can!

For the Christian, the key to life and to development is love. The Apostle Paul listed virtues and spiritual gifts one by one and said that each was worthless without love (1 Cor. 13). Jesus offered a new commandment to His disciples: that they should love one another (John 13:34). A commandment to love? The *principle* of love gives meaning to the Bible. Love is the basic principle for the Christian's moral value judgments.

8

How *Why* Develops

"Why? Mommy, why?" How weary parents can become of this question. Children ask "Why?" partly because they discover that it is a good way to stall for time and partly because they really want to know. At least, they will ask until they are turned off, temporarily or permanently.

"Why?" is a beautiful human question. When you ask, "Why?" you are making an important claim on being a person. *Why* shows belief in purpose. *Why* says that you want to share anything that anyone else knows about what lies beyond the obvious. *Why* shows self-respect: you believe that you are capable of understanding.

Daddy, why are there clouds? Daddy, wny is the dog barking? Daddy, why must I go to bed? Whether the question can be answered with scientific facts, personal opinions or concrete reasons, *Why* helps people get together. It provides a good basis for sharing experiences.

Neither mental nor moral development is just a matter of storing lots of good answers in your memory. Development depends much more on learning to ask important questions. Real development means learning to recognize issues and seeing what needs to be explored. It also means committing yourself to using your understanding and knowledge to solve the problems that confront you.

Four Factors in Mental Development

To better understand how the moral judgment process develops, let's look at the factors involved in mental development—the overall process of which moral judgment is one part.

Again we turn to the research of Jean Piaget. He has found four factors that account for mental development. Each of these is important to parents. Indeed, each of us can gain self-understanding and perhaps get some new ideas about relating to others from the study of these points.

1. Heredity and maturation. The child has inherited the genetic material of mankind. The patterns of development are built into each person. Of course, what is built in is only a broad outline of when and how certain growth will occur. The normal child will get taller, but how tall?

In the mental realm, the child will develop capabilities for abstract thoughts and artistic creativity. Just how strong will these capabilities be? To what extent will the abilities be used? For these answers we must look to the other three factors. Genetic emergence (heredity) is an important factor in development, but it is not one that we can control.

2. Experience. Our knowledge and understanding is based on our own experiences. Experience plays a very important part in development. Parents should be concerned with providing a variety and depth of experiences for the child. Children feel more a part of the family by sharing experiences with the rest of the family. If the experiences of the adults and the children in the family have very little overlap, the family will lack unity.

Experience, in the sense used here, is concerned with *doing* things, not just watching or listening. Especially in the younger child, active play and sports are important. Through doing things *in* the world and doing things *to* the world, we develop understanding of that world.

Remember, the world that a person knows best is the world

he or she reconstructs in his or her own mind. The reality that counts is the reality of one's own perceptions. Only through much experience can this perception grow into a thorough grasp of life.

3. *Social transaction.* Experiences of dealing with people form a special category. Each person is shaped by the understanding that comes from relating to other people. In the animal realm, development involves doing exactly what other creatures of that species do. Behaviors of the "family" members blend together because the range of tasks and roles is very small.

Human development is different. The range of possible human activities is vast. As we develop, we become not more alike but more unalike. Therefore, the probability of our getting in each other's way would be expected to increase. But it doesn't.

Instead, the growing person is a participant in a process called socialization. Through socialization (becoming a more social, interdependent person) we develop behaviors and outlooks similar to those of people around us. In these social experiences, we are affected as much by what *we* do to others as by what *they* do to us. In other words, we are not shaped or molded as if we were lumps of clay.

Let's compare social interaction to catching and throwing a ball. Muscles are strengthened not because of what the ball does but because of what the person does to the ball. With this in mind, it is easier to see why the same experience has different effects on different people.

As we relate to other people, we are affected by the process. What we do and say within a relationship has its effects on our understanding and on our interpersonal skills. Thus we can see how one good experience leads to another—and how one bad experience is apt to lead to another bad experience.

All of us, but especially children, need many opportunities for contacts with other people. Through these social encounters our self-understanding develops. We discover the relationships that are constructive and effective—for our own benefit and for others.

4. Equilibration. Life is full of experiences that don't quite fit into our normal patterns. When these little surprises come along, we don't know what to do. These bumps and swerves are not always comfortable. But if everything in life were easy and predictable, not much development would result. So much of development depends on stretching open our viewpoints to assimilate new ideas. Often, we need to change the shape of our understanding in order to accommodate facts that don't quite fit the old molds.

Even as a bicycle rider leans and sways, the developing person is pushed from side to side in his or her thinking. Riding a bicycle isn't a matter of keeping it rock-solid steady. It's a matter of equilibrium.

Development of understanding and judgment is pushed forward in a similar way: an experience pushes us, threatening our balance. We push back, trying to find a new balance point. Then another unpredictable experience comes along; the process continues. The tendency of the normal human is to find some way to regain stability and to develop because of the jolts and surprises.

Sometimes our concern for others causes us to protect them from every rough spot in life. To do so runs the risk of slowing down development. We shouldn't try to create problems for each other. But we need to see the importance of each person dealing with life firsthand. Did you ever try to ride a bicycle for someone else? Worse yet, picture a father running alongside the bicycle while his son pedals—the father never quite letting go, the son never quite learning.

Four Factors in Moral Development

Moral judgment develops through almost the same processes. Kohlberg has identified four factors that contribute to the development of moral judgment.

1. Experiences of justice. Susan had never understood justice. Then one day she and her classmates played a game in which the opportunity to win depended on having dark hair. Susan became angry because she saw how unfair it was to be a loser because of her blonde hair. She learned the difference between justice and injustice.

Much of what we learn about morality, we learn from the moral environment in which we spend our time. People who are treated fairly usually develop faster than those who experience constant injustice. If we are respected, we discover the value of respect and tend to treat others with respect. If we are treated with fairness and honesty, we tend to treat others in the same manner. But if we are treated unfairly and dishonestly, we will be more likely to show the same unfairness to others.

Nothing has more influence on the development of moral judgment than participation in a just environment. But your view of justice changes as development occurs. To a child in the first level of development, justice has a self-centered meaning. It means not doing more than one's own share, or being allowed to do what someone else is doing.

During this time, the older family members need patience and understanding as the child begins to knowingly ask and answer questions about fairness. The time invested in bridging the gap between the child's view and the adult's view is not wasted. Rather, it is but a small price to pay in helping the child grasp the real meaning of justice.

2. Experiences of social interaction. Social experience has much to do with moral development. People who avoid contacts with others are likely to develop more slowly. The key is that we gain in moral judgment as we become more familiar with other perspectives. Consider this extreme: if you had never encountered other viewpoints, you would likely think of your own as the only possible viewpoint—and thus you would have had no experience in defending it or even explaining it.

Some well-intentioned parents slow down their children by keeping them well insulated from other children who might be a bad influence on them. It is important for any of us, children or adults, to be concerned about the company we keep. But to some extent we *need* to experience different viewpoints, including differences in moral convictions.

Until Bobby met Roger, it never occurred to him that throwing rocks through windows in the vacant house could be such fun. But when Roger hid from passersby, Bobby began to wonder. "Why is Roger afraid of people, Mother?" That question opened up a deeper understanding for Bobby—of Roger and of himself. Without the experience, the conversation would have been meaningless.

3. Open discussion of moral concerns. "It's wrong because I say so, and let's don't hear any more of it." This statement is one of the surest ways to retard moral judgment.

God gave us a marvelous capacity for communication. Using language well is one of the great open doors of development. Moral conscience is a natural tendency; but moral judgment depends on sharpening one's awareness and sharing ideas about meaning. This sharing takes place through discussion.

We should encourage each other to think and talk about the moral implications of the experiences around us. Under no circumstances should a child be turned off when he or she wants to talk about why something is right or wrong. Instead, every member of the family should work toward making it easy to share and to ask questions honestly and openly. A family environment that allows for easy exchange of ideas will help in everyone's moral development, not just the children's.

Bobby's mother knew better than to scold for the window breaking. She valued the fact that Bobby had come to her with his moral concern. She made it easy for him to talk about it.

4. Opportunities for role playing. A person is many things: a daughter (or son), a sister (or brother), a mother (or father), and perhaps a gardener, baker, driver, doctor, salesperson and more. If you stop to think about it, you can recall how much fun it was when you began your childhood role playing experiences. We drive bulldozers, fly airplanes, act on the stage. We play traffic cop, teacher, football star, music director, and photographer. We try on all sorts of roles. Through role playing, we begin to search out a place for ourselves as grown-ups. But we also are discovering ourselves, and thus we get a basis for understanding others. The more experience we have in taking on the roles of others, the more our moral development is stimulated.

Every week or so Jill discovers something new about herself. Most of these discoveries come while she is "trying on" something. In the attic there is a box of old clothes, in the garage, some small tools. Jill and her brothers play house, store, farm, highway repair, and dozens of other do-it-yourself situations. Even more important, Jill has discovered that she is a daughter, a sister, and a friend. Jill is learning to appreciate Jill.

Family life helps a child see the importance of the roles he or she has in the family. A child can see the value in being a friend and sharer of confidences with brothers and sisters; a child can share in decisions, and be given responsibilities. Through these experiences in role playing, along with discovering the consequences of actions taken in the roles, a child develops the sense of responsibility which is a basic part of moral development.

The Task of Parents

Christian parents are aware that they are and should be involved in the moral development of their children. The question is, How to help? Some things will do more harm than good. The moral influence of a parent is a complicated matter.

Children need encouragement and correction. In the years that moral judgment is only partially formed within a child, he or she needs reminders and coaching, lest the childish behavior become seriously antisocial and destructive. How can parents exert moral influence? Rewards and punishments have their place. Use them sparingly—and with gentle kindness, or they will lose their effectiveness.

Later on, behavior problems are more likely to come from gaps between moral judgment and moral action. How can parents have a positive effect on the moral actions of the maturing child? Rewards and punishments can outlast their usefulness. Sometimes examples, models, and fair rules are more effective.

To discipline effectively involves engaging in some act, short of controlling another person, that has a positive effect on the person's self-responsibility. At best, to discipline is to have positive moral influence. The approach to discipline should vary according to each person's level of moral judgment.

As moral judgment begns to develop in the child, it is highly ego-based. What is right is what feels right; what is wrong is what works to the child's hurt or disadvantage. Here is the period when rewards and punishments have their greatest effects in communicating moral influence.

When the child gains enough mental capability to grasp other people's viewpoints, the focus of moral judgment moves outside the self and *others* become important as the source of moral authority. At this time the child begins to lose responsiveness to rewards and punishments and takes on an increased alertness to models and examples. Further in this second level of moral judgment, the orderliness that comes through rules and regulations becomes important. The developing person, usually adolescent or adult by now, takes on a high degree of responsiveness to clearly defined and just rules and regulations.

Those who develop into the principled-justice-level of moral judgment (Kohlberg's Level III) lose some of their responsiveness to the moral influence of models and rules. Transactions and dialogues with other people become more important as a mode of moral influence.

Kinds of Moral Influence
Following is a chart of the strong moral influences at each

level of moral development. The three levels of moral judgment are represented as zones, from left to right. The three levels are periods when each of the three major modes of moral influence are predicted to have their greatest influence. The first mode, rewards and punishments, relates best to people who are making moral judgments in terms of Level I. In Level II, models and rules are most effective. The third mode, dialogue and interpersonal transaction, is most effective for people who are in Level III.

THE STRONG MORAL INFLUENCES AT EACH LEVEL OF MORAL JUDGMENT

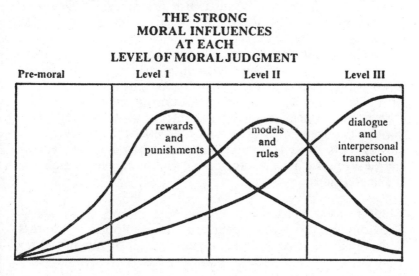

Several practical implications can be seen here. For example, who would be expected to respond best to a Sunday School attendance contest with its typical pay-offs? Who is apt to be least influenced by a discussion of the moral implications of honesty? Who is most likely to be disinterested in a memory verse chart with gold and silver stars? Who is most apt to be influenced by reading an exciting biography or thrilling testimony? Who is most likely to be watching the example you set? Perhaps all of us should think over our own life history and see if we can remember when we were at one of the early peaks of moral development.

Think of it also in terms of religious development: Who is most inclined to respond to threats of God's wrath? Who is most concerned about doing what Jesus would do? Who is most satisfied that "if God has said so, that settles it"? Who is most enthusiastic about daily fellowship with God, willingly and eagerly entered into?

In order that a mode of moral influence be available when needed, it must be "phased in." You can't suddenly turn off one mode and turn on the next. For example, dialogue may not have much influence for the small child, but it should begin early in life.

The chart does not suggest that we lose all of our abilities to respond to any of the earlier modes of moral influence. Even people who judge right and wrong in terms of principled justice might still flinch if a punishment is profoundly threatening. Piaget says that we bring all of our previous capabilities along with us as "checked baggage" through life. But parents must recognize that what has a great deal of moral influence at one stage of life will likely have much less influence later.

Limitations of Modeling

Providing a consistent model (example) is important. Parents soon realize that consistency is hard. If all of our moral influences were limited to the examples we set, we would likely fail.

But children can grow up to be even more moral than their parents. All of us are capable of developing beyond the models we have encountered in parents and teachers. Anyone can continue to develop a higher structure of moral judgment if the opportunity for dialogue and social interaction is available. As far as the family is concerned, what is most important? Being on good terms with every family member.

Developing the basis for dialogue and interpersonal transactions is an investment that should begin early. It is never too early to engage a child in simple reasoning about right and wrong. Reasoning may not have much effect in Level I and not much more in Level II, but you can't wait until Level III arrives to start. The relationship between the parent and the child has to have within it the fundamental respect and acceptance that will provide a basis for mature dialogue and transaction.

Many parents ask for help in building a relationship with a child in trouble. The rapport that is so hard to build in bad times should have been established in good times—but it didn't seem needed then; the child was so obedient and responsive.

Suggestions for the Family

The family should be a just and moral community. Family members are more important than the house or the furnishings or wealth. Family members need mutual respect and a shared concern for righteousness. To maintain the proper moral tone, there must be a continuing concern for the quality of justice in the family. Each member participates in the quest. Try these suggestions in your family to promote the proper moral climate:

1. Discuss moral matters in order to increase awareness of life's moral and ethical decisions.

2. Participate in the improvement of justice in the home and family. To do this, each person needs a sense of involvement in the family's decision-making.

3. Read together and discuss the Bible and Bible stories to become familiar with authoritative moral and spiritual teachings.

4. Talk over your personal experiences and development, with special emphasis on matters of *Why*.

9

What Does God Want?

Part of being human is learning to take the complexities of life and to set priorities. From among the things that God values and wants us to value, we need to find the most important and study them. This chapter suggests four things that God wants: that we accept responsibility, we love Him, we obey Him, and have faith in Him. In terms of your awareness of your own life, which of these are most important? Which need more attention?

People Who Are Responsible

God made us able to make moral choices. Life is full of moral matters. Each person's moral choices are influenced by many factors. But when a choice is made, the person who made the choice is responsible. Responsibility is a value among God's people.

Lately it has become popular to evade the responsibility for moral choices in a great game of passing the buck. We have come to recognize how important environment and influences from other people can be. We see that what we do is determined mainly by what we have already experienced and learned. Thus it becomes easy to push this awareness into an argument that no one should be held responsible for anything he says or does.

People laughed about this tendency in the 1950s when *Westside Story's* Officer Krupke was told that the juvenile delinquent's problems should be blamed on society. By the late 1970s it was no longer a laughing matter.

Recently this argument received added attention. It was the basis of defense cases for murder in Florida and rape in California. Defense attorneys put the blame on television. The defendants killed because they had seen so much killing that they no longer considered it wrong. Thus, the key legal element for a criminal act—ability to discriminate between right and wrong—was missing.

Such a view of moral responsibility has one major flaw. It assumes that the human being has a moral conscience as blank as a new recording tape. The experiences of life make images on this tape, and whatever one does with the resulting sense of right and wrong is no more than a playback of the tape. Such a view leaves us with the sad prospect of having no way to determine anyone's responsibility for anything. Yet God has created in us not only the ability to make moral decisions, but also a basic sense to distinguish between good and evil.

People Who Love Him

What does God want? God wants people to love Him. More precisely, God wants people to *choose* to love Him. Ever since the Garden of Eden, God has been restoring His relationship with human beings. God, the just and righteous Creator of the universe, has also been active as the Redeemer. Redeeming (buying back something that has been lost) is necessary because of sin. God's righteousness hates sin; God's justice requires punishment for sin. But God's love provides a way for people, no matter how sinful, to find fellowship with Himself. "For God so loved the world that He gave His only begotten Son, that whoever believes in Him should not perish, but have eternal life" (John 3:16). Love is a value among God's people.

Two doctrines, God as Creator and God as Redeemer, are the foundations of Christian faith. All that we are and all that we value as good are based on these two beliefs. Thus we value beauty, because God created it. We value nature because God created it. We value truth because, in what He made and what He has said in His Word, God is Truth. He gives us truthful pictures of reality. He does not mislead or confuse us. We value people and our relationships with people because God made them, and no matter how distorted by sin a person may be, God still loves him or her and so should we.

Indeed, love is at the center of these values—a special kind of love, not the trite and selfish love so popular in the world today. The Bible says there are two ways we know we are in God's love: we keep God's commandments (1 John 5:2) and we love one another (1 John 4:21).

People Who Are Obedient

Obedience to God's Word and to God's will is very important. The Christian knows that a life of morality depends on obedience. Since what is moral is defined by the principles of God's Law, obedience to God's Law (or to the principles of the Law) is the way of morality and moral life. When Jesus said, "I am the Way" (John 14:6), He was referring, in part, to the life of obedience. Obedience is a value among God's people.

Beyond the matter of living a moral life, the Christian knows that happiness and success are also dependent on obedience. For the Christian, life's purpose is defined and determined in terms of glorifying God. Whatever glorifies God and honors Him carries with it the by-product of personal success and fulfillment. Unlike the secular person, the Christian should not value material success and power as primary goals.

Indeed, we suspect that even for secular people, success and power are goals that are always beyond reach. The closer one gets, the farther away the goal seems. If wealth is the measure of success, it always takes a little bit more to be really successful. If power and authority are measures of success, one never has enough.

Happiness as a goal is even more difficult to achieve. What produces happiness is less a matter of "big" things than of the little sparkling jewels of moment-by-moment experiences. I have seen people at their "finest hour," receiving high honors in recognition for great achievements, turning from the applause to their persistent sadness.

I know a professor who is recognized worldwide. For his research on heredity he was honored in Stockholm. But he would have traded it all for a second chance with his wife and children. When he lost them, he suddenly woke up to the tragedy that his neglect had created. The "lifts" of life are few and far between for those whose values are locked into themselves. Their sadness runs deep.

On the other hand, I have been among people who end each day in bone-tired weariness, those for whom life seems to hold no recognition and little material reward. Some of these "little" people of God's kingdom have an abiding peace and sense of worth. Their actions and their contributions are known best to God. His approval is reward enough.

Christians are sometimes accused of being "other-worldly." Are we really so preoccupied with life hereafter that we can't keep our minds on things here? Indeed, some Christians use their eternal security as an emotional escape. Others see everything in terms of eternity and thus they fail to take their present responsibilities seriously. That's not what God intended.

The Christian has a blessed hope that gives life greater meaning. Beyond this life there is an eternal life of fellowship with the saints of all time in the presence of our Lord Jesus Christ. This reality is a great underlining of the value of obedience. We obey Christ because we are involved with Him in an eternal fellowship.

Obedience is at the heart of our relationship with God. Happiness and success are values that make no sense to the

Christian apart from God's will. This may sound as if Christianity were locked into Level II moral judgment: response to moral authority from outside in the form of examples, rules, and regulations. Indeed, Kohlberg and others have seen Christianity just this way.

But Kohlberg points out that the basic values of life are seen differently at each level. In Level I, obedience is a matter of avoiding punishment and striving for reward. Goodness, in this view of obedience, is conforming to whatever demands have clout. Obedience, in Level I terms, has the tone of *forced* obedience.

In Level II, obedience means recognizing and willingly putting oneself under subjection to external authority. Examples, rules, and laws are accepted as the basis for an orderly moral life. Those who study such things see religion, in general, working this way. As a person becomes more religious he or she becomes more obedient to the examples, rules, and laws of the particular religious teaching.

God's Word reminds us, "Yes, you have heard it said by your religious leaders that the law of God says all of this, and that is good as far as it goes, but I say unto you . . ." (Note how similar is Jesus' teaching in Matthew 5:21-48). Then, the Bible emphasizes not rules, but principles: "If you really had understood what God wants, you would know that it is not obedience to God's Law as to rules, but obedience to God's Law as to principles as, for example, mercy, compassion, love—concern for people!" (Note the contrast Jesus made in Matthew 9:13 and 12:7.)

In Level III obedience is not forced (as in Level I) or willing (as in Level II), so much as it is natural. Obedience in Level III comes out of a relationship. It is a response of a loving involvement, a deep fellowship—oneness.

"Your wish is my command." Only to a person whose trust you share deeply can you say this and really mean it. When two people grow together, they make their decisions more and more together. So it is with our relationship with Jesus Christ. Obedience becomes an essential part of the relationship we have with Him.

Christ is our Master. In Level I, this matter of being a servant of God likely has an element of fear and forced service about it. In Level II it has an element of compliance and legalism about it. But the great revelation that comes with moral maturity is that our experience as God's servant changes our perspective. No longer is it a matter that we *must* serve God or even that we *ought* to serve God, but that it is *natural* that we serve God—we have a new nature. By faith we walk with God.

God is transforming us, bringing into us the mind of Christ—who, knowing full well that He was in power and authority, put all of it aside in order to become a servant, fulfilling God's will even to the sacrifice of His life; after this, God highly exalted Him (Phil. 2:5-11). God wants us to value obedience as Jesus did. Not because we must be obedient or that we ought to be obedient, but that in our natures' being transformed we *are* obedient to God.

Obedience, Trust, and Faith
In the transformed life of mature Christian experience, obedience is hand-in-hand with trust. As we learn to trust God obedience becomes firm. The emergence of obedience and trust says much about the quality of faith. Following is a chart in which the relationship is suggested.

People Who Have Faith
"Do not be anxious for tomorrow" (Matt. 6:34).

Amazing, isn't it, that some Christians can be such anxious, uptight people. Jesus taught that His followers should live a day at a time, not fretting about what might happen. In fact, the teaching of Jesus in Luke 12:22-34 sounds like a good excuse for not doing much planning. But rare is the Christian who doesn't get anxious from time to time.

In some ways it is easier for a non-Christian to be relaxed about important matters. When basic values are involved, the Christian is more apt to see the life-changing possibilities and

The Development of
Obedience, Trust, and Faith

Levels of Moral Judgment	Obedience	Trust	Faith
Level I	Obedience emerges	— —	Confidence of consequences
Level II	Obedience is firm	Trust emerges	Belief in God's law as rules for behavior
Level III	Obedience is natural	Trust is firm	Faith in God's Law as principles for personal relationship (with God and with others)

to be concerned about them. For example, whether a young person takes God into account in making some of life's major decisions is of great concern to Christian parents. The education or vocational training a person chooses will increase or decrease his or her sensitivity to God's calling for life vocation.

Decisions about marriage—whether to get married, to whom, why, and when—have profound effects on the quality of life and the spiritual welfare of the person. How one uses his or her time, from late childhood on, has a great influence on the contribution one will make to others and on the worth of life itself.

Since the Christian assumes that life has purpose and that certain outcomes of life are more valuable than others, all of these decisions are important. They may be important to some non-Christians, as well, but the Christian is far more apt to see beyond the immediate outcomes, especially to see beyond short-term happiness and to be concerned in a deeply serious way.

Is it right for Christians to be so intense and so serious? Does that reflect the depth of faith Jesus teaches us to have? Once again, a specific teaching of the Bible seems to be somewhat inconsistent with the realities of a godly life. We must keep things in perspective.

The idea, "don't be concerned about tomorrow," is not an absolute so much as a comparison. Compared with the planning that a person without faith must do (or at least *should* do) if he or she is even half aware of the hazards that lie around the corner, the Christian's approach to preparing and planning is a combination of faith and action. The difference is the *faith* factor.

Trust for Tomorrow

Because a child of God has faith, tomorrow's burdens can wait until tomorrow. A Christian rarely has any good reason to lose sleep fretting. God will provide. "My grace is sufficient for you" (2 Cor. 12:9). For Christians, planning is a matter of doing today what God sets before us. In faith, we know that today *is* the preparation for tomorrow.

When a burden of unfinished work or a sense of unpreparedness keeps me from sleep, I see it as a kind reminder and an invitation from God. Almost always, such fretful nights come after a time when I have been making careless choices. My priorities have become sloppy. Instead of using my time and energy to do only the most important things, I have been trying to do everything, all at once. So when I try to sleep, God keeps me awake—kindly reminding me to get back into the *valuing* business. I must take responsibility for making my own choices. God wants me to get my moral self back into action—to think through the unfinished work and the demands of tomorrow and decide what is most important. It can't possibly be everything.

When my life gets so jammed up with fretting that I can't even sleep, I get up quietly and make a list. I list the things that I am concerned about. Then I write down practical steps that I could take to deal with each problem. It takes time, but it feels better than tossing and turning in bed.

The list is step one. Next, I prayerfully think about the importance of each item. I ask God to help me see the really important matters and set my priorities. It isn't numbness or less concern that I need; it is perspective.

When I've arranged my priorities, I copy the list again and put the important items at the top. What works for me might or might not be useful for you. Nevertheless, I testify with confidence: God has never delayed in answering my prayers for a restored sense of values.

Sleeplessness, or some other signal that something is wrong, could be God's way of giving you a kind reminder and a gentle invitation. The *reminder*: Life is better when you keep first things first. Decisions about priorities are at the heart of being fully human. The *invitation*: No matter how hopeless the pile of responsibilites and unfinished work may appear, getting things back to a healthy condition begins with making choices on the basis of values. Make your list. Prayerfully find the most important matters, and take at least one practical step toward the one or two that are most important.

We need not fret over tomorrow; we can live today with God's priorities and know we will be adequate for tomorrow. God wants us to be responsible, yet not anxious or pushy. God wants us to love Him because we choose to. God wants us to obey Him because of our fellowship with Him. God wants us to have faith in Him—a faith that deepens because of trust and obedience.

10

When Values Are in Conflict

All sorts of trivial matters lead to clashes. But in this chapter the focus is on conflicts of moral values. What values are important enough to concern us? What can parents do to encourage the development of these values? What can be done when we see another person "going wrong"? What are the dangers of a conflict in values?

Don't Fence Me In!
High fences don't keep weeds out of a garden. How does a gardener handle weeds? With the hoe, the gardener gently roots them out. He feeds the good growth and discourages the bad.

Putting up protective barriers around small children helps keep them from wandering into the street. A fence also helps keep stray dogs from bothering them. But fences are useful for only a few years.

Parents can't keep children inside the fences forever. The human being develops through exploring. Moral values are not developed through meaningless rituals and habits. They are developed through thoughtful choices about moral matters. If there is freedom to choose, there must be freedom to make a bad choice. Where there is no freedom to choose, there is no freedom to learn.

God made us to be creatures with moral judgment (content and structure make up moral judgment). Because of this, He enabled us to deal with the reality of evil. Where did evil come from? Why did God allow the presence of evil in the Garden of Eden? It had to be. Could Adam and Eve really share in (or even recognize) God's moral character without facing moral choices?

Chapter 3 of the Book of Genesis shows us that. Eve was impressionable. Perhaps she was even a bit gullible. No matter how much she may have wanted to believe God and to please Him, she tended to doubt Him. She was willing to take a chance on a different moral choice.

Adam showed these same traits, yet he went one step further. When confronted by his error, he tried to shift the responsibility. Sin makes us quick to transfer our moral responsibilities. That way we don't have to face up to sin as a reality. The Apostle James wrote that we are tempted to sin when we are "carried away" by our own lusts (James 1:14).

The Genesis account begins the long saga of God's actions to bring us back into fellowship with Himself. God provided a solution for sin. The short-term solution was in animal sacrifices. These sacrifices provided the needed covering for the guilt. They also provided a basis of obedience and symbolized man's need to place himself at God's mercy because of sin. The long-term solution became clear when Jesus Christ fulfilled the conditions of the death penalty on behalf of all who believe.

The Christian's moral righteousness does not depend on doing good works in order to earn merit and favor with God. Instead, our relationship to God depends on Christ's righteousness. "He [God] made Him [Christ] who knew no sin to be sin on our behalf, that we might become the righteousness of God in Him" (2 Cor. 5:21).

God accepts the Christian as being without sin. Since the penalty for sin has been paid by Jesus Christ, the guilt of sin has been removed "as far as the East is from the West" for those who belong to Christ. God knows that His children continue to sin. For this He makes provision. He accepts us in a process of continuing forgiveness, not because of our good intentions, but because of Christ.

Through Christ we enter into a special relationship with God called a *new birth* and *adoption*. Becoming part of God's family brings about a change in values. For some, the evidence of this value change is soon in coming. In others, it is a slow process, so slow that sometimes onlookers become skeptical.

God's influence and presence in the life of the Christian (referred to biblically as the indwelling of the Holy Spirit) helps tip the moral balance toward God. Seldom does the Holy Spirit bring about instant moral reform. But just as the first Adam tended to make moral choices *away* from God, the Christian shares in the nature of God's "second Adam" (Jesus Christ) and tends to choose *toward* God's values in moral matters.

God leaves all people free to choose. Those who reject are free to reject. God does not override their decisions and force them into a relationship with Himself. Those who do accept are free to develop slowly or more quickly depending on their daily choices about walking close to God, being fed by His Word, and fellowshiping with others of His people. God doesn't force us into a particular rate of spiritual growth.

God's Example

The Bible uses the word *Father* in many places to describe God's relationships to His people. Sometimes, parents get carried away with this imagery and pose themselves as God-on-earth for their children. For anyone to see himself or herself this way is dangerous. A very faulty view of God can thus be put before children.

God is Creator, Provider, Judge, and Redeemer. When a human being plays God, a sloppy mixture of these characteristics results. The Bible gives us all of these aspects of God. But when it deals with God in very personal terms, the Bible uses the word Father. In these passages, God is the gentle Provider—concerned, protecting, and reliable.

Insofar as the parent represents God, especially in the life of a little child, the representation should show God's gentleness, His patience, His continuing nurture and care. The Holy Scripture faithfully represents Him this way. His is not the vindictive and harshly judgmental parenting that some Christians act out!

God liberates His children, making us free to be real people, free to develop, to explore, to find ourselves and to find His purposes for our lives. Should Christian parents do otherwise? Don't be offended when a young man or woman pleads, "Don't fence me in!" Sometimes it is hard for parents to accept this because they have dreams for their children. Wise parents must take care not to manipulate their children into fulfilling their own dreams.

Compulsive parenting is dangerous. Children should not be driven. The Bible warns that fathers are to keep their children "under control with all dignity" (1 Tim. 3:4). The parent's dignity and the child's dignity are both involved. God's Law is concerned with respect and love as defined by righteousness: "Fathers, do not exasperate your children, that they may lose heart" (Col. 3:21).

When People Go Wrong

How can people who have had all the advantages of a Christian home and family sometimes go wrong? The biblical promise (Prov. 22:6), that when the child is old he or she will not depart from the way, is hard to square with appearances.

What does it mean to "train up a child in the way he shall go"? Does *train up* mean to create in the child a set of mechanical habits? Indeed not. God's nature and His values point to an entirely different meaning of *training*.

Since God has created us as creatures of will and moral choice, He respects our freedom to choose—even if we choose not to believe in His Son. God punishes for the wrong choices, but the freedom to persist in wrong choices is there.

God does not make decisions *for* people. Nor does God force all persons to conform to His will.

Does God ask parents to treat their children as horses or dogs, to be trained to jump through moral and ethical hoops? Notice who responds to the applause after the trained animal act—the trainer! Bringing up children is sometimes similar. Parents who seek applause for their spirituality train their children to do all the right things at the right times—even if they have to violate the integrity of the children in order to "train the act."

God does not ask for an animal show. Instead, God demands a continuous process that consists of far more than rewards and punishment. The process includes setting examples—reliable, continuous examples. It also involves developing a dialogue focused on the motives behind the behavior.

A Very Old Story

Learning to trust God's basic goodness is one evidence of spiritual maturity. Hand in hand with trust is the self-respect that seeks answers: "Why, God? Please show me Your purposes." God has purposes; life is not some wild, unpredictable nightmare. But in order to build our trust, sometimes the answers to our questions come very slowly. This was Job's experience.

In the oldest book of the Bible, God deals with values. Job had all the good things of life. He was a rich man by secular standards (a fine house, land, power, wealth) as well as by standards a Christian can respect: family, self-respect, love. Job was a man of honorable values.

But God's plan for Job was to bring him to a deeper sense of spiritual trust. Job lost everything that seemed important except his relationship to God. Crushed down by physical and emotional suffering, he was indeed a man to be pitied.

His friends weren't much help. They decided that Job was being punished for his evil deeds. Even his wife, rejecting him, looked for an easy answer. Look how God is treating you, and for no good reason! Death itself would be an improvement over your terrible suffering. "Curse God and die!" (Job 2:9) But Job did not.

Instead, he came face to face with God in a deeper sense of trust. Job saw that in God and in His righteousness are the ultimate values of life (Job 42:1-6). Afterward, Job was healed by God and returned to a life of even greater happiness, wealth, and honor. Again, the good things of life that God gave him seemed to vindicate Job as a righteous man.

Is this a story of how the good guys always win in the end? Indeed, no. Job's story reaches its climax at the point when he learned how basic and how adequate is trust in God. This is the high point of triumph even though Job was a penniless, sick, and pitiable man. His triumph was in his trust in God, not in the rewards that followed. Indeed, the good things of life don't always follow. Many are the saints of God whose only reward will be in heaven.

Whose Fault?

Parents make a terrible mistake when they assume too much responsibility for what their children become. God asks nothing beyond our willingness to cooperate in His work in people's lives. He doesn't ask us to take it over, nor does He hold us responsible for what others choose to do with their lives. In love we should show our concern, but we should not burn bridges or cast stones. And we only hurt ourselves by feeling guilty.

Take courage from the story Jesus told of a grown son who chose against his father and against God. He asked for his share of the family inheritance. Apparently, he was old enough to be eligible, yet what an insult to the rest of the family. The father went along with his son's wishes.

As the story unfolds (Luke 15:11-32), it is clear that the father felt that his son was completely lost—virtually dead, at least spiritually. We see only a little of the father's grief. Instead the story is focused on the young man's experiences and his view of himself. As he hit bottom, he reflected on what he had lost. Then he repented and returned. The father had not searched for him. No pleading letters had been written. The son was in God's hands all along. The father's hurt was deep, the longing great. He watched the roadway. One day he spotted his son in the distance. "He's coming back! Thank God!" Every story does not end like this, but God is in control. God loves His children. One of the greatest reassurances we have is that God does not want any to perish but for all to come to repentance (2 Peter 3:9).

Helping in Moral Development
What can parents do? Indeed, what can any of us do for each other that will be helpful in dealing with the conflicts that emerge as we develop? Here are seven tasks that can and should be undertaken:

1. Stimulate inquiry. Moral conflicts cannot be resolved apart from understanding. What is the issue? What is at stake? What are the consequences? We need to stimulate each other's inquiry into these questions. Moral development absolutely depends on it.

2. Stimulate verbalization. Not everyone finds it easy to talk about important things. It's easier to talk about baseball and the weather. But we need to help each other find ways to talk about the moral conflicts we face. This may mean enlarging the vocabulary, especially in dealing with children. Without the use of language to share and to discuss, moral development is slowed severely.

3. Ask "why?" Children should try to find their own answers to this question. Moral conflicts and moral development respond to the deeper look at *why*. "Never mind that we disagree," you might say, "just tell me why you see it that way." Seeking understanding comes first; seeking agreement should *follow*.

4. Provide experiences in which issues are examined. People who are developing together, as in a family, need common experiences. In order to talk about moral aspects of life you need to share similar experiences. Acts of kindness shared together, such as visiting the sick or bereaved, taking flowers to a neighbor, or working together, make sense even to small children, *if* they are discussed and the moral issues are made clear. Experience and discussion of the good side of life provide the skills needed when the rough spots of conflict must be resolved.

5. *Dialogue (listen responsively).* Moral conflicts respond best to honest dialogue. Conflicts are rarely resolved by speech-making. Even if only one person is wrong, the process of communication demands that all involved have a chance to be heard. We all need to develop the skill of listening responsively. The secret is to *listen* instead of planning your reply. When you do say something, make sure you're responding to what the other person has said.

6. *Explore disequilibrium. Disequilibrium* means realizing that your basic beliefs seem inadequate. It occurs at several points in normal moral development. It sounds like this: "Dad, I've always believed that God made the world and that He is interested in me, but I'm really wondering now." The temptation is to hide such heresy under the rug. "But, Bill, you can't possibly mean that." Stop! Try this instead: "You've got some things to think through. Let's talk. Why don't you tell me how you're looking at it now?" Exploring *with* the person is far more helpful than trying to correct the person.

7. *Stand alongside.* When all is said and done, it's being there that counts the most. The Holy Spirit stands alongside as the presence of God with us. Even so, the major contribution we can make to others, especially within the family, is to stand alongside—even in times of conflict.

11

The Conflicts Ahead

Religious freedom runs deep in our historical tradition. For many who first came to North America from Europe, freedom to worship God in their own way was extremely important. Even while America was still a group of British colonies, the reputation of this continent was established. Here was a safe haven for persecuted Christians.

Christian Nations?
The United States and Canada have been called Christian nations mainly because of their tendency to consider Christian values. In their governments and in their homes, the people of these nations have been seen as basically Christian.

Historians don't all agree that calling either the United States or Canada a Christian nation is accurate, but the tradition is there. Freedom to worship God has been a cornerstone in their development.

Too Easy! One unfortunate by-product of living in a "Christian" nation is that we tend to take religion for granted. We become flabby Christians. Just as one's body needs exercise, one's religious beliefs need to be put to work—and the tougher the going, the stronger we become.

Flabbiness and sloppiness are not pleasing to God. God did

not intend for us to sit and watch life go by. Jesus said to His disciples, "You are the salt of the earth; but if the salt has become tasteless, how will it be made salty again? It is good for nothing" (Matt. 5:13).

Christians are to stand for something. God's attitude toward no-count Christianity is also revealed in these words to the church at Laodicea, "I know your deeds, that you are neither cold nor hot. . . . So because you are lukewarm, and neither hot nor cold, I will spit you out of My mouth" (Rev. 3:15-16).

Where Christians don't really stand for anything and where there are few pressures on the church, a soft and mushy Christian experience results. Then God allows persecution to move in. At times like these the church, again and again through history, has toughened up and stood for something. The text in Revelation about the church at Laodicea illustrates this idea: "Those whom I love, I reprove and discipline; be zealous therefore, and repent. . . . He who overcomes, I will grant to him to sit down with Me on My throne" (Rev. 3:19-21).

Conflict is necessary to strengthen the church in the world. The great moments of forward movement of the church have often followed after persecution. Such a period may be about to break in upon us.

Family at Issue

Among the issues likely to cause friction in the near future, the Christian view of family values is close to the top of the list. Three points distinguish this position.

First, in the Christian community the family cannot be abandoned; it is basic. Second, the Christian family is now well on the way to being distinctly different from the secular family (or whatever substitute for the family secular society may create). Finally, the pressure of secular society on this increasingly different family—the Christian family—can have certain strengthening outcomes for the church.

Complaining about television may be useless, but the grow-

ing number of programs that scoff at the family alarm me.
Those programs that get people more accustomed to the idea
of fatherless families and casual living arrangements are part
of the pressure already mentioned. A values battle is getting
under way focused on matters of the family. Christians now
have a clear-cut chance to stand for something.

In addition to these family related values, other matters
seem ripe for large-scale conflict. Notice how many of the
items mentioned under "Secularism" are already matters of
house-cleaning within the church.

Secularism
Secularism describes the human condition apart from God.
When we refer to the secular society, we mean the non-
Christian majority of mankind, including the institutions,
customs, and standards by which people live in ignorance or
rejection of God.

Crucial secular values are *self-centeredness*, *materialism*,
and *humanism*. (This list of three secular values could be
stretched into dozens of points, described in altogether different terms, or even reduced to one item: sinfulness.) In light
of the research on the development of moral judgment,
secularism can be seen as ungodly evidences of shortcomings
at each of the three different levels of moral judgment.

Self-centeredness is an evidence of Level I's failure. Adults
who have been stunted in their moral judgment still think of
moral choices, as a child does, in self-centered terms. Self-
centeredness is not a choice for such a person: it is the trap in
which the person is caught. These persons don't necessarily
want to be self-centered; many or most can't help themselves.
Everything is good or bad, right or wrong, evil or righteous
according to how it works out for them.

Materialism is the general term that embraces Level II
moral judgments apart from God. In the research studies,
Level II refers to moral judgments made on the basis of standards set by others.

If one does not see God as the basis of the standards, then

two problems occur. First, the standards of society have no clear basis and must be constantly challenged and frequently changed. Second, the standards and rules of society are relative to each situation that comes up. What is right today may be wrong tomorrow.

In this chaos, each person reaches out for something to hold. Since moral standards are not seen as reliable, even human relationships are not trustworthy. What else is there in which to put one's confidence? Things. Possessions, though not necessarily evil in themselves, become the major sin of secular people in Level II of moral judgment.

Preoccupation with possessions and the tendency to treat people as objects indicate materialism. Who can deny that materialism is virtually the modern way of life?

Some materialism is better explained as evidence of selfishness or self-centeredness, and thus it should be seen as Level I judgment. But to suggest that all of the materialism in our society is a matter of selfishness is too simple. Consider the many people who amass great wealth with the intention of using the wealth to help others. Consider even the schools, hospitals, mission organizations, and churches that are dedicated to the service of physical and spiritual needs. How easy it is for them to overemphasize their brick-and-mortar properties that become great monuments to materialism.

When people are limited in their moral judgment to the structure of Level II, they easily fall prey to the materialism that is motivated by human competition. Even in doing humanitarian good works, being preoccupied with what others will value tends toward materialistic activity. (We should not forget that Christians are often caught in these same secular tendencies because of the powerful influences of our society.)

Humanism is the secular form of Level III moral judgment. Without God, principles must be based on humanity itself. Truth, as a principle, is valuable because it is part of the humanistic basis for social trust. Love, as a principle, is valuable because it gives quality to the social experience. For the humanist, the ultimate principle is life itself. Thus, the humanist brings all matters of right and wrong to center around the principle of life. "Reverence for life" some have called it.

The great secular philosophers have wrestled with the principles of life, trying to find its meaning. For better or worse, the value of life itself seems to be the dead end of humanism. Without hope of life beyond the grave, much of the value of mortal life never comes clear. In the words of a dismal secular song, "Is that all there is?" Humanism, as a moral philosophy, provides very few answers to the *Whys?* of life.

Biblical Answers

To respond to these three forms of secularism, we should think in biblical terms. Never forget that these issues face the church and the Christian family too. They aren't just outsiders' problems; they are ours.

Level 1. "And just as you want men to treat you, treat them in the same way" (Luke 6:31). The biblical answer for self-centeredness is very direct. Treat others as you want them to treat you. This is practical advice though it is very difficult for a person who is self-centered. Such a person can tell you what should be done to please himself or herself. "What's in it for me?" is the basic language of self-centeredness. Jesus wisely accepts this starting place and switches the moral obligation so that it works both ways: to *others* as to *you*.

Scholars in the field of moral development point out that this so-called Golden Rule is heavy teaching to expect a child to understand. Indeed, a young child would lack the sense of what it is like to be someone else. Thus, although it is memorized by many youngsters, the full meaning may not come to light until ages 8 to 11.

When Jesus first said it, He said it to adults who needed to hear it—adults who were secularized by the basic human tendency to be self-centered. This tendency to think first of themselves was working against their moral development. They were still morally underdeveloped children.

Does this problem exist today? Indeed, yes. Our society is weakened by the self-centeredness that asks, "What's in it for me?" Being concerned about others is out of style for some people. "If it feels good, do it." "Look out for number one." These are the slogans of many in our secular society. It even gets into the Christian family and into the church in the form of individualism and selfish egotism. Whenever we put our own concerns and interests ahead of our concern for others, it is not pleasing to our Lord.

Level II. "Do not lay up for yourselves treasures upon earth" (Matt. 6:19). The biblical answer to materialism is also very direct. No matter how satisfying, the piling up of wealth is not "where it's at" for Christians. There's nothing wrong with being responsible about providing for one's need and for one's family, but it easily gets out of hand.

As a person gains in material things, he or she gets more concerned about order and protection. When our valuing of law and order is primarily in terms of protection for ourselves and our goods, something is wrong. If we follow Jesus' teaching and devalue material wealth, law and order take on new meaning. We can focus attention on the protection of the rights and welfare of others.

Level III. "I am the Way, and the Truth, and the Life; no one comes to the Father, but through Me," (John 14:6). One of the main concerns of humanism is *truth*. It is the cornerstone of science and the major emphasis of philosophy. What, then, is truth?

Jesus boldly answers, "I am the Truth." He identifies Himself as one with the Godhead in the work of Creation. He is the Source of all that is revealed. Whatever science discovers is because of truth; Christ the co-Creator put it there to be discovered. Whatever mankind creates in the arts, music, and literature is because of truth; Christ the co-Creator put it within men and women to share in true creative arts. Whatever philosophers understand of the truth is possible because of the inherent trueness of God's universe. Thus, through human studies, creative acts, explorations, and experiments, men and women grope toward a grasp of truth. Jesus Christ steps from the fog-draped unknown and announces, "I am the Way, the Truth, and the Life." Christians need not be locked into the groping of humanism. Instead, we can join as competent participants in humanistic activities and pursuits. The great difference is that we know the Person who is the Originator and the Source of whatever is discovered as truth.

The Fall of Tradition

At the practical level, much of the conflict we face comes from the fall of tradition. Since World War II, a drastic change has been taking place. Our traditions are changing.

We have had to make dramatic changes in our thinking recently because of automation, atomic power, a shrinking world, increasing international conflict, terrorism, and the energy shortage. No wonder traditions are falling.

But traditions help to stabilize society. People need to be able to count on something. So when traditions fall, people are confused because they've lost their point of reference.

Consider one example that illustrates this well: the matter of traditional ways to dress—coats, ties, skirts, hats, etc. Arguments about the proper way to dress occur in many families. Dress and the decisions about how to dress appropriately for particular events have become a home battlefield. The conflicts and arguments are only symptoms. The basic issue has to do with traditional versus pragmatic valuing.

A person or a society which decides whether or not something is worthwhile by asking, "Does it work?" or "What is it good for?" is pragmatic. Pragmatism values things, ideas, and people, not because of their own worth but because of what they can *do*.

As our society becomes more pragmatic, it becomes less traditional. Those who hold traditional ways are old-fashioned and thus are in conflict with others who hold for pragmatic ways.

In matters of proper dress (as in many other things), young people tend to make their decisions on the basis of what they believe others will do. "But, Dad, *nobody* wears a tie to church." Nobody? Nobody Bob thinks to be important. Indeed, conformity is a strong factor in most people's decisions about what to wear. The issue of tradition versus pragmatism lies just below the surface: to what is one conforming?

As traditions fall, conformity remains. To what will the Christian be conformed? Surely not the promised secular values:

But realize this, that in the last days difficult times will come. For men will be lovers of self, lovers of money, boastful, arrogant, revilers (abusive), disobedient to parents, ungrateful, unholy, unloving (inhuman), irreconcilable, malicious gossips, without self-control, brutal, haters of good, treacherous, reckless, conceited, lovers of pleasure rather than lovers of God; holding to a form of godliness, although they have denied its power" (2 Tim. 3:1-5).

These values may become ours too if we conform to secular examples, loving "the approval of men rather than the approval of God" (John 12:43). Where will we stand?

12

The Greatest of Values

Christian values? When you add them all up, one word says it: *love.* The principle that Jesus said held together all of God's dealings with mankind, the principle that Jesus emphasized in what He called "a new commandment," the reason for the cross, was love.

Love of God for people, love of the redeemed for God the Saviour, and love of people for each other are the three basic kinds of love. The Bible reveals God acting toward people in love. Even when acting in judgment, God in love made a way for His own people. The Bible shows the happiness and fulfillment that comes to those who love God. The Bible also shows that love for others is the natural outgrowth of God's love for us.

But what is love? Such an overworked word. We hear it thrown around in all sorts of loose ways. It slushes out of radios and stereos; it supposedly explains pathetic happenings in television dramas. It shows up in absurd poems on February 14. Love is a word almost worn out from overuse. Or maybe from misuse, or abuse.

The Bible might even be criticized for overuse of the word. No matter where you slice into it, the Bible talks about and demonstrates love. But the Bible is God's Word, God's message to mankind; and the essence of that message is that God loves and cares for people.

The Source

Where does love come from? Does it just spring up out of nowhere and leap on us when our backs are turned? Hardly. Like most emotions, love is a response. We are most inclined to be loving when we are aware of being loved.

One of the most pleasant experiences in my life has been hiking in the mountains. It's especially great where the mountains are close enough together that hikers on one mountainside can see and hear hikers on the trail on the next mountain. Across the valley will come an echoing distant shout, "AahhLohhh." And you cup your hands beside your mouth and reply, "Hello!" Back and forth several times, no particular message, just the greeting of human beings letting each other in on the joy of life.

Love is that sort of experience. Love is back and forth sharing—often with no particular message—just letting another person in on your joy of living. But who starts the process? If love is a response, who makes the first move?

All love can be traced to one source: God. God, in creating mankind, made Adam and Eve sharers of His own characteristics (the image of God). Thus, the tendency to respond to love with love is a built-in trait. Those who seem to be without any trace of love in their lives are usually those who have had little love shown them by others. But those who show a vast capability of loving are usually reflecting and responding to what they have known from others.

For the Christian, knowing God—the Source of love—should be enough to start the process, even if those nearby aren't showing much love. The Apostle John pulled it together in a very simple statement: "We love Him, because He first loved us" (1 John 4:19).

Knowing About Love. Christians can make a mistake about love. We hear so much about it in sermons and Bible teaching. We must be careful not to think of love as a

thing—something that we just know about.
Jesus loves me, this I know."
Hold it! What do you mean, "Jesus loves me, this I
know"? Try it this way: Jesus loves me, this I *feel*! Not very
good poetry, but it adds the heart to the head. Love is not
only a matter of knowing; it includes *feeling*, as well. It's
reassuring to *know* that you are loved, but it's also important
to feel loved.

But that heads us off in another dangerous direction.
Love, real love, isn't just a warm puppy. It isn't just a fuzzy,
floaty feeling. Love is solid, stubborn, and real. Its reality lies
in the fact that it is both knowing and feeling. At the base of
it, we know God, and thus we know His love. Through His
Word, and through His creation, we know Him.

Kinds of Love
What kinds of human love are there? Motherly love, brother-
ly love, patriotic love, and love for chocolate-covered
doughnuts. There are different kinds of love and in some
languages there are different words for each. The Greek
language of Bible-times used different words for sensual love,
family love, and Godly love. Let's look at love through the
three levels of moral judgment.

Level I Love. The self-centered viewpoint shows up even in
love. Love is real enough, but it doesn't have the other person
at its center. Much sensual love is of this sort. What can I get
out of the relationship? What will I get in return for my acts
of love? If I give, what will I get?

Level II Love. The rule-structured strength of Level II
moral judgment puts some backbone in love. No longer flabby and self-centered, love is disciplined into a sense of duty
and responsibility. Love sees from the loved one's viewpoint.
Love has its do's and don'ts. There is a more orderly set of
boundaries, a set of expectations for oneself and for others.
Here we can say that love has its definition in a sense of
justice and integrity.

Level III Love. The highest form of love which we can

know is to be living within the principle of love itself. Beyond all the sense of duty, beyond the concern for responsibilities, and the mechanical aspects of give and take, love becomes a state of being. Love is the way you are.

It is hard to frustrate Level III love. It doesn't stop to say, "That's not fair!" It doesn't resent the moments of distance and frustration. It depends not on the terms of the relationship but on the relationship itself.

Love in Level III is a state of inner peace. The peace "passes all understanding"; it is not something you simply believe, but something you confidently know is in you. Because of your love relationship, you have been transformed. You share yourself with others, and they become part of you. In His prayer for us, Jesus found these words to describe this:

> "I do not ask in behalf of these alone, but for those also who believe in Me through their word; that they may all be one; even as Thou, Father, art in Me, and I in Thee, that they also may be in Us. . . . I in them and Thou in Me, that they may be perfected in unity, that the world may know that Thou didst send Me, and didst love them, even as Thou didst love Me . . . . that the love wherewith Thou didst love Me may be in them, and I in them" (John 17:20-26).

Tend My Sheep"

Love is active. It is not just a state of being, such as being smart or having red hair. Love is something that you live out. Love is something that you *do*.

Jesus was trying hard to rebuild a relationship of trust with the Apostle Peter. Not many days before, Peter had abandoned Jesus when He most needed a friend. Peter had saved his own skin by swearing that he had never known Jesus. Making matters worse, Peter recalled that he had promised Jesus he would never be unfaithful, and he felt desperately guilty about it. So Jesus gave Peter a chance to renew their relationship of love (John 21:15-17).

"Do you love Me?" Jesus asked. "Yes, Lord, You know I do," Peter replied. What followed shows the sort of action that firms up love: "Tend My sheep." Jesus asked Peter not only to say it, but to act on it. In this case, Peter's grief and guilt were so overwhelming that at first he was not able to claim the deep love that Jesus was talking about. Instead, Peter used a simpler word for love. Never mind—Jesus seemed to say—make your love active, put it to work, and it will grow. "Tend My sheep."

Smothering Love
A good gardener will sharply warn, "Don't water it too much." In watering a plant, as in much of life, enough is enough; more is too much. How much love is too much?

If God's love is any example, there is no such thing as too much love. God's love is boundless. But we sometimes show love in unhealthy ways. Even the idea of good deeds can go sour. Once there was a cartoon showing a Boy Scout helping the legendary little old lady get across the street. But since in this case she didn't want to go across that particular street, she was kicking and screaming.

If we aren't alert to other people's needs and interests, we can impose loving acts upon them. Sometimes we smother people with loving acts of the wrong sorts.

The most dangerous of these is overprotection. Parents are particularly apt to run into this problem, but sometimes even husbands and wives do. It is indeed loving to have concern, and even to be fearful for the welfare of a loved one at certain times. But there is no way that any of us can live another's life for him or her. We have to give people growing room and space to explore. Remember that where there's no chance to make a mistake, there's no chance to learn.

Oneness is a value of marriage, but the Christian model for oneness is the relationship of Christ and the church (the bride of Christ). Through the ages, Christ has been building His church, as He promised, but the church and Christ still have separate identities. Wives and husbands too should develop their separate identities. Mothers and fathers should let children develop their own identities.

We are not so many peas in a pod. We are people. We have personalities. No two of us are exactly alike. We are being conformed to the image of Christ, but we need to be careful not to shortcut that process and expect another Christian, even a family member, to be conformed to us. That sort of love smothers development.

The Sign of Love

People like to wear signs—not necessarily big signs, but signs, nevertheless. Consider the little cogwheel of the Rotary Club; the blue and gold "L" of the Lions Club; the two-eared jug of the Gideons. Oh, how nice it is to let people know who we are.

How do you let people know that you belong to Jesus Christ? Wear a little gold cross, of course. Will that do it? Perhaps it will offer a clue, but it is surely not good proof. The Bible says there is a sign of love among Christians; and it is not a gold cross on a chain or pin.

"By this the children of God and the children of the devil are obvious; any one who does not practice righteousness is not of God, nor the one who does not love his brother. For this is the message which you have heard from the beginning, that we should love one another" (1 John 3:10-11).

For the Christian, the sign of love is a two-part sign. One part shows our love relationship with God. The other part is in the showing of love for our "brother." When the Apostle John used the word "brother," it is likely that he meant our brothers and sisters in Christ. Each of the two parts of the sign depends on the other part. Either part alone is incomplete.

"By this we know that we love the children of God, when we love God and observe His commandments" (1 John 5:2). "And this commandment we have from Him, that the one who loves God should love his brother also" (1 John 4:21). Putting it more bluntly, "If someone says, 'I love God,' and hates his brother, he is a liar" (1 John 4:20).

Remember that Jesus taught no restrictions on love: "Love your enemies, and pray for those who persecute you" (Matt. 5:44). "Do good to those who hate you, bless those who curse you, pray for those who mistreat you" (Luke 6:27-28).

The Apostle John reminds us that love starts at home. Our first concern is among those in the family. What sense does it make to show love outside the family if we can't be loving within the family? It may be easier to appear to be loving with someone you don't live with. The little things that rub us the wrong way are bearable, and sometimes not even noticed in a series of short-term encounters. But those we are with day in and day out—that's another story. All the little flaws, habits, and mannerisms can irritate, unmercifully it seems. And that's where the principle of love in its full maturity comes in:

Love is patient, love is kind, love is not jealous, love does not brag. It is not arrogant or rude. Love does not insist on its own way; it is not irritable or resentful; it does not rejoice at another being wronged; but rejoices in the right and with the truth. Love bears all things, believes all things, hopes all things, endures all things. Love never ends (author's paraphrase, from 1 Cor. 13:4-8).

Practice these things at home, and they will become more natural among fellow Christians, at school, in the market, at work, and among those who need to know our Saviour.

The Bottom Line

Where should a book on values end? Of all the important values of Christian experiences—values in the person, values in relationships, values in skills, competencies, abilities— we must decide what is most important. Being human means making decisions and setting priorities.

If I am eloquent in speaking and writing,
If I have gifts of prophecy, scientific understanding, knowledge from vast libraries, even great faith, Without love these are noisy, worthless, nothing. The real values

of time and eternity will stand. There are three: faith, hope, and love. But the greatest value is love. (Author's paraphrase from 1 Cor. 13.)

Glossary

Abstract, as in *an abstract idea.* Concerned with theoretical and background matters; although a thing might be beautiful, beauty is abstract; if it's abstract, you can't touch it; contrast with *concrete.*

Action, as in *moral action.* The doing of something; the *act* itself; behavior.

Aesthetic, as in *aesthetic values.* Concerned with beauty, grace, elegance; taste in matters of art, music and literature shows aesthetic values.

Belief, as in *religious belief.* What one holds to be true; a strongly held belief is a conviction.

Concrete, as in *a concrete idea.* Concerned with things or people that are "here and now"; anything "concrete" is solid enough to sit on, hold, or point at while you talk about it; contrast with *abstract.*

Consistent, as in *consistent response.* A response, reply, or action that is the same or very similar each time one reacts to the particular situation; such a person is being consistent.

Content, as in *the content of a moral judgment.* The matter of *what* is judged moral good or bad; e.g., "lying is wrong" is a content; contrast with *structure.*

Discipline, as in *a discipline problem.* Behavior, especially in the sense of controlled, orderly behavior; also refers to the process of controlling behavior; one is either self-disciplined or can expect to be disciplined.

Equilibration, as used by Piaget to refer to one important development process. The process of getting one's understanding "balanced out" again after encountering an idea or experience that doesn't fit into what one already believes.

Ethical, as in *an ethical problem.* Concerned with right and wrong; especially moral standards for human conduct.

Ethics, as in *a matter of ethics.* Concerned with the recognized and morally accepted standards of behavior.

Extended family. A cultural variation of family style in which people of several generations live together as one unit, usually involving grandparents as well as children who are cousins.

Formal operations. Refers to thought processes that are advanced; able to think abstract thoughts and to reason about complex matters.

Inconsistency. Unpredictable; makes observers uneasy because there is lack of pattern and logic in the behavior; contrast with consistency.

Judgment, as in *moral judgment.* The mental processes by which a person decides whether or not a given act or value is good or bad, right or wrong. The judgment process has two parts: content and structure.

Moral, as in *moral judgment.* Concerned with good and evil, not simply personal taste or preference; moral issues are, for a Christian, concerned with sin and righteousness; humanists and Christians generally agree that when a decision or choice involves the welfare of one or more human beings, it involves moral judgments.

Nuclear family. Based on the idea of a center of nucleus, the nuclear family is one that centers around the mother and father; usually refers to the parents and children until their marriage. Nuclear family images are those most commonly associated with "family" in mass media and conversation in middle class United States and Canada.

Operations, as in *mental operations.* The processes of thinking: recalling, associating, reasoning, judging, etc.; used in reference to Piaget's conclusions to distinguish between concrete operations and formal operations, i.e., thinking about things verses thinking about ideas.

Perception. The mental process in which things observed are converted into meanings—usually described as connecting the recall of previous experience with the thing being currently observed, e.g., a person *sees* an object moving across the scene, the mind *perceives* it to be a horse.

Quest, as in *quest for justice.* A search and the effort to build or help to build what is being hunted; a quest is sometimes a lifetime commitment to seek out and to value, e.g., quest for truth.

Self-Understanding. Becoming conscious of oneself in terms of positive and negative characteristics, strengths and weaknesses, tendencies and values; includes realistic appreciation and valuing of one's own worth.

Sensorimotor, as in *sensorimotor learning.* The use of muscles, activity and the physical reaction systems as the basis for learning; as in infancy and early childhood, the child discovers earliest impressions of the world by kicking against crib slats, rubbing blankets, snuggling up to warm flesh, and by putting things into the mouth; sensori: sense-oriented; motor: muscular movement.

Structure, as in *the structure of a moral judgment.* The basis on which a content of moral judgment is held to be true and important; *why* one believes something is right or wrong; a matter of deep probing—simple statements about "why it is wrong" or "why it is right" are usually extensions of one's content, e.g., "It's wrong because God says so" is a content statement; "God is final judge" is more likely a matter of structure.

Taste, as in *matters of taste and preference.* The simple preferences or choices in matters of custom (e.g., dress and hair style) or of aesthetics (e.g., what is good and beautiful in art and literature).

Values, as in *moral values.* The choices, investments, and purposes which reflect a person's lifestyle and personal commitment; in moral matters, what a person holds to be right and wrong.

Bibliography

Bryan, James. "How Parents Teach Hypocrisy," *Psychology Today*, 1969, vol. 3, no. 7.

Elkind, David. Exploitation and Generational Conflict. *Journal of Educational Research*, 1969, vol. 62 (10).

Hartshorne, Hugh, and May, Mark. *Studies in the Nature of Character: Volume 1, Studies in Deceit.* New York: Macmillan, 1928.

Hoke, Donald E. (ed.) *Evangelicals Face the Future.* South Pasadena, CA: William Carey Library, 1978.

Keniston, Kenneth (and the Carnegie Council on Children). *All Our Children--The American Family under Pressure.*

Kohlberg, Lawrence. The Development of Children's Orientations toward a Moral Order. Part 1: Sequence in the Development of Moral Thought. *Vita Humana* 6:11-33, 1963.

Kohlberg, Lawrence. Early' Education: A Cognitive-developmental View. *Child Development.* 39:1013-1062, December, 1968.

Kohlberg, Lawrence, and Mayer, Rochelle. Development as the Aim of Education. *Harvard Educational Review.* Vol. 42, No. 4, 1972.

Kohlberg, Lawrence, and Turiel, Elliot. "Moral Development and Moral Education." In G. Lesser (ed.), *Psychology and Educational Practice.* Chicago: Scott, Foresman, 1971.

Maslow, Abraham H. *Motivation and Personality.* New York: Harper, 1954. 2nd ed. 1970.

Olthuis, James H. *I Pledge You My Troth: Marriage, Family, Friendship.* New York: Harper and Row, 1975.

Piaget, Jean, and Inhelder, Barbel. *Psychology of the Child.* New York: Basic Books, 1969.

Prior, Kenneth F.W. *The Gospel in a Pagan Society.* Downers Grove, Ill.: InterVarsity Press, 1975.

Selman, Robert. The Relation of Role-taking to the Development of Moral Judgment in Children. *Child Development,* 42:79-92, 1971.

Stone, Lawrence. *The Family, Sex and Marriage in England* 1500-1800. New York: Harper and Row, 1977.

Woodward, Kenneth L.; Lord, Mary; Maier, Frank; Foote, Donna M., and Malamud, Phyllis. "Saving the Family," *Newsweek.* May 15, 1978.

Wren, Brian. *Education for Justice.* Maryknoll, New York: Orbis Books, 1977.

Wynne, Edward A. *Growing up Suburban.* Austin: University of Texas Press, 1977.